OPTIONS TRADING MADE SIMPLE

HOW TO BUY CALLS & PUTS AND ACHIEVE FINANCIAL
FREEDOM IN ONLY 5 YEARS

LEARN STOCK OPTIONS TRADING SERIES: VOLUME 1

TRAVIS WILKERSON

HTTP://WWW.TRADERTRAVIS.COM

CONTENTS

HOW TO GET THE MOST OUT OF
THIS BOOK

If you want more details than what's included in this book, I highly recommend you view, for FREE, the bonus package I created for readers of the book.

You'll gain access to the following:

- A seven-module option basics video course.
- A video case study of the two strategies taught in this book. You'll see how a U.S. investing champion trades and makes decisions in real time.
- You'll also gain access to my trade journal excel. This way, you can see the history of my trades and what positions I'm currently in.

Along with your case study, you'll also get my emails, where I share my favorite option trading strategies, ways to protect your investments in any market, and complimentary alerts about trades I'm going to place.

All of these bonuses are 100% free, with no strings attached. You only need to enter your email address. To get your bonuses, go to:

https://www.tradertravis.com/bookbonus.html

Or scan the QR code below:

INTRODUCTION

> "In our view, however, derivatives [options] are
> financial weapons of mass destruction, carrying
> dangers that, while now latent, are potentially
> lethal."

> — BERKSHIRE HATHAWAY INC. 2002 ANNUAL
> REPORT

A recent National Institute on Retirement Security
(NIRS) study stated that the average retirement account
balance is $3,000 for all working-age households and
$12,000 for near-retirement families (Rhee, 2013).
That's not enough to live on in retirement! This
sobering reality is one of the many reasons people are

trapped in their 9-5 job and feel hopeless about the future.

In my experience, options trading is the perfect solution to this dilemma. It's a leveraged way to invest in the stock market and can quickly turn small sums of money into large amounts. You can also use them to generate consistent income each month or even insure or protect the value of your investment account. Best of all, any investor (not just billionaires) can use options.

Speaking of billionaires, did you know that Warren Buffett, one of the world's wealthiest buy-and-hold investors, referred to options (aka derivatives) as "weapons of mass destruction." The irony of this statement is that he used options to make $7.5 Million, and he didn't have to buy a single stock share to earn that. A few years later, he would again use options to generate $4.9 billion in income.

It's a classic case of doing as rich people do, not as they say. Options have been Buffett's secret weapon for generating income for more than 30 years. Yet, most investors have never heard of options, much less used them. And the few who discover their potential are usually told to avoid them by some uninformed financial professional.

Not using options in your overall investment plan would be a colossal mistake, but to be fair, there is something of which you should be mindful. The benefits and possibilities aren't the issues. The problem is that **options can be risky if you misuse them;** hence Buffett called them "weapons of mass destruction."

Another important note, the educational waters of this industry are treacherous and strategically designed to complicate the learning process. You must safely swim from point A to point B while avoiding the hungry guru sharks trained to eat your wallet for lunch. Maybe you've seen many of their outrageous claims?

> *"With this secret strategy, I took $2,000 and turned it into a million in a year; I make 10% a month on my money, and I can teach you how to do the same; Would you like to (fill in the blank)?"*

Essentially, their claims boil down to one thing: you'll generate instant and easy cash with a few clicks of a button. Claims of turning $2,000 into a million within a year easily seduce wannabe investors, and sadly, seduction sells. It speaks to the irrational nature inside of us. The side that makes us buy into "get rich quick" schemes even though we know they aren't true.

So, what about you? If faced with two paths, the easy (fast) option or the more challenging (slower) option, which would you choose? This is not a trick question. I promise. It would be no surprise if you chose the easy/fast choice. I would guess that 99% of people would prefer that option. It's human nature. Honestly, who wants the hard/slow route?

Fast, easy profits are the "holy grail" people search for. It's irresistible, especially early on. I know because I initially chose the quick, easy path. Therein lies the big problem. Quick profits don't play well with the journey to building wealth. The two concepts are oil and water, and I'm not the only one who has discovered this. Sam, a student whose name and details have been changed to protect his identity, was also seduced by the allure of getting rich quickly.

When I first met Sam, he couldn't keep up with the rising costs of goods and services no matter how hard he worked. He never seemed to make enough to get ahead.

Sam and his wife Sara listened to the "experts" and put their money into mutual funds. For years, they watched their account go up and down in value. After ten years, their balances were essentially the same as when they first started (the lost decade). That's a lousy way to make money, and they felt trapped.

He and his wife were getting closer and closer to the end of their working life and just wanted to know how to manage their investments themselves. They also knew they couldn't survive another market crash. This is why options appealed to them. They needed something to provide profit in both up and down markets.

Ultimately, they were trying to bolster their dwindling retirement accounts so they could enjoy retirement without stressing over money. Sam used the tools taught in this book to generate over $47,000 in profits. And in the following pages, you will discover precisely how they achieved just that.

You'll also discover the blueprint I used to achieve financial freedom. And when I show you this five-year retirement plan, the blueprint Sam learned, I want you to be mindful of something. You may be like me when you first see it and think, *No way it's this simple. It has to be more complicated than this.* If so, that's normal.

A little bit of skepticism is healthy. I, too, was skeptical when I first started. I didn't believe the plan would work, so I quasi-implemented it. After one year, I realized it really did work! From that point on, I was all in. My wife and I focused 100% of our efforts on the plan, and after five years of sacrifice, we were able to kiss our corporate careers bye-bye, and we haven't returned since.

So, after two decades of trading and winning the U.S. Investing Championship, I decided to write the book I needed when I started my journey—one that makes options trading simple! I've taken everything I've learned in my 20+ years of trading and provided the easiest path for beginners to travel. You'll discover my favorite 10-minute trading strategy that gives growth and market crash protection.

Of course, I can't promise you'll achieve the same results as Sam and me. But I promise to show you what has worked for me and the steps I've taken to earn additional income, protect my investments, and experience freedom in my life.

Here's to YOUR future success,

Trader Travis Wilkerson

10-Minute Income Trader ™ & founder of https://www.tradertravis.com.

1

BENEFITS, BASICS, AND TRAPS OF OPTIONS TRADING

> *"In the hands of a skilled surgeon, a scalpel is a powerful tool that saves lives. In the hands of a child, it can be an effective way to lose a finger or worse. Options are the financial equivalent of a scalpel.* **Used appropriately, options can be a highly effective way for investors to manage risk."**
>
> — FORBES.COM ARTICLE [EMPHASIS MY OWN]

The stock market is risky, but when used correctly, options trading can reduce overall investment risk and provide a steady stream of retirement income. However, you must be wary of a common pitfall—choosing the path of easy riches.

People searching for easy riches seek wealth creation with little to no work. If you succeed and make easy money, it often leaves just as quickly because you didn't build the character traits of a successful person. Two of those traits, in particular, are discipline and patience.

You see, wealth is like a long-term successful relationship. Harder to achieve but worth it. So, you have to decide on the front end. Do you want to chase the fantasy of getting rich quickly, or do you want a proven wealth blueprint?

If you want a proven blueprint, like Sam and Sara, then you're in luck. That's precisely what I'll share in this book. They weren't unrealistic, and that is what I liked about them. They weren't obsessed with getting rich quickly. They just wanted a strategy that worked. But let me back up as I'm leaving out a vital piece of their story.

Like most, Sam was initially attracted to the fact that you can double or triple your money with options. Having reached his 50s, he wanted to speed up his retirement date. Sam worked in the public sector and hated his job. Well, hate is such a strong word. Let's put it this way: his career didn't fulfill him.

He was tired of living paycheck to paycheck and putting vacations on credit cards. It was frustrating to want out of the corporate rat race while knowing their 401ks wouldn't allow them to retire comfortably.

Sam and Sara had followed the advice of the buy-and-hold experts, yet their real-world results were much different from the hypothetical returns they bought into at the beginning of their careers. Their goals had been reasonable: earn an extra $2,000–3,000 a month.

The couple had always dreamed that, once they retired, they would take a trip to Europe and visit Venice, Italy, to enjoy the honeymoon they never took 31 years ago when they married. An extra $2,000–3,000 a month would have allowed them to do that.

They had heard that becoming a real estate investor was an excellent way to become wealthy, but who had the time for that? They were busy professionals and didn't have time to deal with tenants. Their next bet was the stock market. They went to a one-day promotional seminar to learn about options trading.

They were told it was easy to learn and they'd need less startup capital than real estate. They were also impressed by the "cherry-picked" examples of trades with a return on investment of 100% or more. But what really got them was this: A $100,000 options portfolio that promised 30% yearly returns would produce $2,500 of monthly income. If the money were left in the account to compound for ten years, it would grow to $1.3 million.

That was precisely what they were looking for! However, they didn't buy the expensive seminar course but instead went to the internet and searched "how to trade options." Faced with a million search results, all promising instant, easy riches, they were intimidated and nervous.

They didn't know where to start but, more importantly, whom to trust. It didn't take long before Sam and Sara found themselves $10,000 in credit card debt from buying too many "shiny objects." They had blown through what little savings they had. Things weren't looking good. They were pretty close to just throwing in the towel. But that's when it happened ...

I'll finish their story later because you need to understand precisely why Sam and Sara invested $10,000 yet still didn't know how to be successful options traders. Sadly, it's all too common, and if you understand the why, you can avoid the same trap.

If you've been researching the topic of options trading for any length of time, you have, most likely, discovered that many gurus and professionals don't explain options trading in simple terms you understand. This unnecessary complication frustrated me until one of my millionaire mentors shared his conspiracy theory with me.

Initially trained as a salesman, he gave me his inside perspective on how things work. Please keep in mind that this was just his opinion. It doesn't make it true or false. He said the financial industry intentionally complicates straightforward concepts. If learning about options trading is hard, then one of two things usually happens.

Scenario 1: You will throw up your hands in frustration and conclude that investing is too hard. You'll start believing the hype about giving your money to a professional to manage.

OR...

Scenario 2: You start to believe it's complicated because you don't have the "solution." Note: It's easier to sell someone a solution if you make things complicated. This solution is usually in the form of an investing course.

The challenge is that things are still not clear once you buy the course. So when you ask them questions, they say you need more training. Then, they proceed to upsell you into more expensive classes. The longer you stay in the dark, the longer they can sell you solutions.

So, that's the trap Sam and Sara were caught in—an educational trap. I, too, experienced this, and my goal with this book is to help you avoid that costly experience.

As a beginner, your most significant hurdle to becoming a successful options trader is learning the basics of stock options. The technical details about options basics can be tedious and uninteresting. However, you must know the basics to achieve the rewards. It's the price you pay for options greatness.

I'm speaking from experience. Options trading allowed me to achieve financial freedom and leave corporate America when I was only 34. However, the process of learning about options made me feel dumb.

I stayed dazed and confused for six straight months before the concepts started to make sense. This is also why I got caught up in the educational swamp of snake oil salesman. They kept telling me there was an easier way, that their simple strategies were the only method I needed. They lied!

I've been trading options for several decades, coached thousands of traders, and haven't found a shortcut. You must slog through the dry, dull, and technical details. Those who give up and go off in search of quick and easy are always the ones that fail.

For that reason, there are more failure stories than success stories. The people I've seen fail are those who never took the time to master the basics. All the advanced strategies are nothing more than the basics applied.

Here's another success tip: those who win with options are not always the smartest or the ones with the best tools. Those that succeed do so because they are the most disciplined. And once you see the returns you can earn, you'll understand why people have difficulty being disciplined with their money.

> *"Investing is not a game where the guy with the 160 IQ beats the guy with the 130 IQ. Once you have ordinary intelligence, what you need is the temperament to control the urges that get other people into trouble."*

— WARREN BUFFETT

All in all, learning and mastering the basics of options is worth it! So don't give up. After all, it's a skill that empowers investors who are tired of losing money in the stock market to consistently earn 2%–5% each month (without being glued to the computer all day).

Right about now, you may be saying, "Yeah, right." I admit it does sound too good to be true. But it is true, and I completely understand how you feel. I'm skeptical by nature, so even I thought it sounded farfetched. However, I was fortunate to have a millionaire mentor teach me about this alternative form of investing and prove that it was real. It's the secret tool of the ultra-wealthy.

The more common and less profitable investing methods are known by many. You can invest in bonds, stocks, or commodities. But the more lucrative and relatively unknown way to invest in the stock market is through stock options or options for short. A few benefits of options trading are:

- Options allow you to benefit from a rise or fall in a stock's price without actually owning the stock.
- They also allow you to make money when the stock market goes up, down, or sideways.

- Lastly, they are leveraged. A 1% gain in a stock's price can often produce a 10% gain in the options contract attached to that stock.

So the options market runs parallel and is tied to the movement of the stock market. If you have a basic understanding of the stock market, picking up options shouldn't be too much of a problem. With that being said, let's go over five subtopics that will take you through the basics of trading options:

1. Stock Shares Compared to Stock Option Contracts
2. Options Buying Versus Options Selling
3. The Four Components of a Stock Options Contract
4. How Options Traders Can Double Their Money Quickly
5. Tips on Opening an Options Account

STOCK "SHARES" VERSUS STOCK OPTION "CONTRACTS"

When you own stock or shares of a company, you own a small piece of the company—you're an owner. When that company's value goes up in price, so do your shares, and you have the opportunity to sell your stock back into the open market at a higher price.

However, a stock option doesn't give you ownership of anything. It's instead an agreement or contract between two parties. One party agrees to deliver something, in this case, stock shares, to another person within a specific time frame and for a particular price.

These contracts are also attached to a specific stock, so the contract price and the stock share price move in unison, but the option's value moves at a magnified rate.

Said another way, the value or price of that contract will move at an accelerated pace compared to whatever percentage change the stock experiences. When the stock has a 1% move in price, the option contract can have a 10% move in price (up or down).

OPTIONS BUYING AND OPTIONS SELLING

There are two parallel approaches to trading options. You can be an options "buyer" or an options "seller." Most traders sell options for monthly income. However, the tradeoff is your profit is often capped or limited. Selling options will take a book in and of itself, so I will only cover buying stock options in this book.

When you buy an option, your profit is usually unlimited, and you can often make a 50% to 100% return on your money in a matter of weeks, if not days. I know how unbelievable that sounds, but stick with me, and you'll see how true it is. Later, I'll teach you a "proof of concept strategy" so you can verify these earnings claims yourself. However, it's essential for you to paper trade the strategy. Paper trading is where you go through all the motions of investing with options, but you don't use real money.

It's also called virtual trading. One of the many reasons you paper trade first is because *"options are the financial equivalent of a scalpel."* It's a cautious approach that ensures you learn how to use the tool correctly. Never risk real money until you understand what you are doing. You don't want to lose money unnecessarily. Most Brokers also take this careful approach regarding approving you to trade options on their platform.

STOCK OPTION CONTRACTS

In the old days, option contract terms were made up individually, making it easier for someone to be taken advantage of. Eventually, they were standardized and regulated, meaning the contract terms were the same across the board. It's now a fair and level playing field, which is good news for us.

Warning! I will introduce some technical jargon, but I'll simplify it later with examples. The primary vehicle behind options trading is something called a stock option contract. For simplicity, I will refer to options on stocks only, even though options can be traded on commodities and other securities.

Whether you buy or sell an option, it is a legal contract insured by the Options Clearing Corporation (OCC). They guarantee that the terms of the agreement will be honored.

There are only two types of options: call options and put options, also known as puts and calls. Every single options strategy is a variation or combination of these two.

- The **call** option gives its buyer the right, but not the obligation, to **buy** shares of a stock at a specified price on or before a given date.
- The **put** option gives its buyer the right, but not the obligation, to **sell** shares of a stock at a specified price on or before a given date.

There are also two types of calls and puts: American-style or European. I will mainly discuss American-style options in this book. With American-style options, you can exercise your right to buy or sell the stock any time before the option expires. European-style options can only be exercised on the expiration day.

> The Boring Technical Definition of a Stock Option: If you buy or own one stock option contract, it gives you the **right, not the obligation,** to **buy or sell** 100 shares at a **set price** on or before a **given date** (time period).

> A Simpler Definition of an Option Contract: Options give you the right to buy or sell a stock at a specific price and for a limited time. When the rights of the option contract are exercised, the set or specific price of the stock can be bought or sold at is called the **strike price**.

A stock option contract is composed of the following four components:

1. underlying security or stock
2. the right, not the obligation, to buy or sell a stock
3. a specified price for the stock (strike price)
4. a fixed time for which the option is valid

For example, if the contract was for an **IBM, 2022 May 50 call option**

1. IBM is the underlying stock.
2. The call gives the owner the right to buy the stock.
3. The strike price is 50, so the owner would buy IBM for $50 a share.
4. This option contract is valid until May 2022 (a fixed time).

If this May 2022, 50 call option were exercised, the option owner would buy 100 shares of IBM stock for $50 a share. They could do this anytime, but they only have until May 2022 to exercise these rights.

A quick mental break! Options trading is very involved and can be pretty complex, but I will try to make things as simple as possible. For now, don't stress about getting a complete understanding; that will come with time. Just read for comprehension, not a thorough understanding. Moving on ...

A stock option contract grants you the right to buy or sell a specific stock, but you can only do so for a specified time because options eventually expire. Unlike stocks, options contracts have an expiration date; after this date, your contract expires, and your option ceases to exist.

Translation: They disappear from the inventory of contracts available to trade. Options are often called wasting assets because of their expiration dates. Stock options contracts are like most contracts; they are only valid for a set period.

So, if it's February 2022 and you buy a June 2022 option, it is only suitable for four more months. The contract will expire or cease to exist in June, and when it expires, you forfeit the rights granted by the contract. You also lose the money you paid for the option; this is what they mean when they say an option expires as "worthless." Its value drops to zero.

Option Expiration Date Analogy: I have a contract with a local gym. It gives me the right to go to the gym whenever I want, but I'm not obligated. They don't make me go, but if I don't exercise my right to go to the gym, I lose the money I paid for this right. After a year, my gym contract ends, and I no longer have the right to work out at that gym. Unfortunately, this seems to be the case. It's pretty silly how my wife and I keep a gym membership even though we don't go. Anyway, back to the lesson …

You don't have to buy or sell the stock if you don't want to. However, if you don't exercise the rights of your contract, you lose the money paid for it.

Also, when you are looking to buy an option contract, you might see a small amount, such as $1.50, listed as the price. To arrive at the actual cost of the option ($150), multiply the quoted price by 100 because one stock option contract equals or represents 100 shares of a company's stock. When you buy one contract, you purchase the right (not the obligation) to buy or sell 100 shares of that stock.

Before we move on to how traders (also known as speculators) double their money with options, it's crucial to understand how buy-and-hold investors use options. The concept of options has been around for ages, even during biblical times. In the U.S., however, the first options market began in 1791 when the New York Stock Exchange (NYSE) opened. Thus began the "wild west" of options trading. Then, in the 1970s, options became more mainstream and standardized.

Back then, an investor could call their broker and say they were "bullish" on a particular stock and wanted to buy a call option. Bullish meant they thought the stock would increase in price. However, instead of tying up thousands of dollars buying stock shares, they could invest a small sum to buy a call.

For example, buying 100 shares of stock XYZ @ $150 would cost the above investor $15,000. If they were right about their bullish stance, they would profit. If they were wrong, they could potentially lose all $15,000. A cheaper way for the investor to benefit from the bullish outlook was through an options contract.

The investor could buy a 6-month 150 call option on stock XYZ for $10 ($10 X 100 = $1,000). This would give them the right to buy stock XYZ for $150 for the following 6-months. If the stock went up to $160 or more, they would make money and could exercise the call to buy the stock at the 150 strike price. If the stock didn't rise in price, the most they would have lost is the $1,000 they initially paid for the call, which is much less than the $15,000 it would have cost to buy the stock. In summary, call options are a way for investors to place cheap bets on the direction of a particular stock without actually buying the stock upfront.

Okay, enough of the boring technical details. Let's move on to the fun stuff—discussing how traders can double or triple their money in weeks, if not days.

HOW TRADERS DOUBLE THEIR MONEY IN A FEW DAYS TO WEEKS

A person can make so much money with options trading because of "financial leverage." On the surface, that makes no sense to someone new to the concept and certainly doesn't show you *how* to make money. Let me walk you through an example of leverage in action. I'm going to do it with an actual trade I made.

On 11/6/09, I bought an options contract for about $600. Buying 100 shares of the stock would have cost me upwards of $10,000, but for a smaller sum of money, I could control and still benefit from the movement of the stock shares. Remember, options allow you to benefit from a rise or fall in a stock's price without owning the stock.

I looked into my account roughly six days later, and that trade was worth about $3,300. Since I'm no fool, I took my profits and ran. After paying fees, I made a $2,700 profit in only six days.

The quick, accelerated gains I made on that trade are why people are eager to learn how to trade options!

Everyone dreams of getting rich quickly (even if we know it's impossible). Again, it is financial leverage that makes options trading so powerful and allows for such returns. You can multiply small sums of money into more enormous sums of money.

Another example of leverage you may be familiar with is buying homes. Let's pretend I was a real estate investor and found a house worth $50,000. Then, I signed a contract to buy it within the next three years. With most real estate contracts, you have to put some money down; they usually call it earnest money. Let's say I put down $500.

That's leverage. A small sum of money gives me access to an expensive asset, and I can potentially benefit from that asset going up in value. The contract gives me the right, not the obligation, to buy the home. It's like a call option for houses.

Now, let's pretend they built a golf course near that home, and the home's value increased to $80,000. I would then have a contract that says I could buy an $80,000 house for $50,000, and I only put down $500 as a good faith deposit. In this example, I have a contract that allows me to buy something at a significant discount. If you understand that, you can understand options trading, at least the buying side.

Remember, if I were to buy the house (exercise the terms of the contract), I would need $50,000. Only then could I sell it for $80,000 and realize the profit. Or I could exercise another option and take the approach of an options trader.

I could take my purchase contract and sell it to someone else. My contract would be more valuable than when I purchased it because the underlying asset attached to it increased in value. If I were to sell the contract to someone else, I wouldn't need $50,000 to realize a profit (that alone is why I'm an options trader).

Maybe I could find another investor and say, "Hey, I'll sell you the rights of this contract for $5,000." It's a no-brainer for them because they will still have lots of equity in the home even after buying my contract. I paid $500 for the contract but sold it for $5,000. The $4,500 profit equals a 900% return on my money.

By the way, this happens all the time in real estate investing. I know because I used to be a real estate investor. Notice I said, "used to be." That's a long story filled with drama and ends in personal bankruptcy. That failure motivated me to pursue options trading, but I'll have to save that story for another time. I don't feel like reliving that agony right now. Back to my example ...

The 900% return on my money is the leverage. I risked losing $500 to make $4,500. Said another way, I bet a small amount of money to achieve a much larger profit.

The small amount of money allows you to get into the game. Paying $50,000 for a house and then selling it for $80,000 is the equivalent of investing in stocks. You need more money to get ahead. However, with options trading, the financial investment required is much smaller.

That's a short example of how you can make money by buying and selling a contract. An options trader performs the same transaction, but the underlying asset is a stock, not a house.

- Real estate investors buy and sell homes.
- Stock investors buy and sell shares of stock.
- Options traders buy and sell contracts.

Options traders make money when the price of the contract they buy increases. When that happens, they sell their contract back into the open market at a higher price than they paid.

They purchase and resell stock option contracts all the time. This is because minor stock price fluctuations can significantly impact an option's price. If the value of an option increases sufficiently, it often makes sense to sell for a quick profit.

Do you want to know something that is not common knowledge? Warren Buffett, via Berkshire Hathaway, uses options in his overall investment strategy. You can verify this by reviewing his 13D filings or reading shareholder letters.

Let's get back to buying and selling contracts for a profit. The concept usually doesn't make sense to new traders, and, honestly, it won't make complete sense until you've put it to practice in real life. I want you to think on a surface level. Many people make the mistake of trying to comprehend options trading in one sitting, which is not possible.

Forget about trying to understand how you can make money with contracts. Just understand this: Options trading is nothing but the buying and selling of contracts. Understand that on a surface level, and then everything you learn after this will build upon that.

In the next section, we will cover the essential tools of options trading—put and call options (also called puts and calls). You'll also hear the second half of Sam and Sara's story because those tools are what allowed them to experience freedom in their life.

CALL & PUT OPTIONS BASICS

Earlier you were introduced to Sam and Sara, two average individuals who used options to earn over $47,000 in profits. Before I get into the boring details of puts and calls, let me finish their story. Where were we? Okay, I remember …

Sam and Sara were $10K in credit card debt from being suckered into buying too many "shiny objects" (aka options courses). They had blown through much of their meager savings and were close to throwing in the towel.

On top of that, Sam and Sara didn't realize who they were up against. Most experts who own these websites and write these books are former Wall Street professionals. Granted, they are knowledgeable, but is it just me who thinks they aren't blessed with the gift of explaining things simply?

Each year the ability to make money in the stock market gets harder and harder as more and more people enter the ring. Today the competition is insane, and information overload keeps you stuck! It's dog-eat-dog out there, and it's becoming a nightmare for people like you, me, Sam, and Sara. They were about to throw in the towel. Then, they ended up on the website of a guy whose message instantly "connected" with them: (http://www.TraderTravis.com).

Sam and Sara figured they'd give it one last shot. They had nothing to lose. They emailed him, not expecting to hear back. What happened next changed their lives. Seriously, their results were simply amazing!

All they did was use the same two simple tools other stock market millionaires use—puts and calls. As the financial author Dave Ramsey said, "If you do rich people stuff, eventually you will be rich. If you do poor people stuff, you will eventually be poor." Mr. Ramsey can sometimes be controversial, but I have to agree with him on this one.

So, what are puts and calls? Generally speaking,

- Put options are used to protect the value of your assets and make money when stocks fall in price.
- Call options are how investors profit from rising stocks, but they make ten times more money than buy-and-hold.

As the buyer of an option, it's not uncommon to earn (or lose) upwards of 40% to 50%. But one of the inherent problems with options trading is that these returns seem too good to be true for new traders.

Where else will you hear it's possible to make $2,700 in six days? It's not like they teach you this stuff in school. And with any other form of stock market investing, you don't have these returns in such a short period. So, it's natural if you are a little skeptical; so was I.

The problem is that these kinds of returns are typical. They can happen regularly if you develop the right skills. But what many people choose to do is succumb to their skepticism. They avoid this life-changing information when it could help them. This is especially true for people who don't have $30,000 to invest in stocks. Yes, there is a risk with trading options, and you won't always make money, but the rewards are well worth the trouble (at least in my experience).

Stock options are precisely what the ultra-rich use for accelerated wealth creation! But what about the ordinary person? What about the person barely scraping by with the dream of becoming wealthy? The answer is simple in concept: do what the rich do. The wealthy people I know either trade or, at the very least, learn about stock options.

These are the tools they use for asset protection and accelerating wealth creation. You can buy a call option and earn supercharged returns on stocks that go up in value. Or you can sell a call option and earn additional income on your stock holdings. (This is done through a covered call strategy.)

You can buy a put option and earn supercharged returns on stocks that go down in value. Or you can buy a "protective" put option to ensure you don't lose money on a stock purchase. On the selling side, you can sell a put option and be paid to buy a stock at a lower price (This is done with cash-secured puts).

I'll cover "buying how-to" later in this book, but I want to introduce you to the benefits of options trading right now. The benefits of options trading will keep you motivated; you will need all the motivation you can muster.

Even though there is a lot to learn, realize that everything boils down to two components: calls and puts. That's it—only two types of stock options! Everything else is just a variation or combination of these two.

While this is just an overview of calls and puts, we will go deeper in the following chapters. For now, know that both are used for asset protection and wealth creation, and you can use them to make money in ANY market environment. Puts and calls are used to do the following:

- Make money when stocks go up in price.
- Make money when stocks go nowhere in price.
- Make money when stocks go down in price.

It's truly a fantastic experience, so I hope you decide to become a successful options trader one day.

BUT...

I know from experience that understanding this concept is challenging. There is so much information to take in. That is why I'm not teaching you any advanced strategies just yet. My focus in this book is on the basics of buying options.

The next primary term to understand is *option chain*: it is a list of all the stock option contracts available for a given security (stock). When you go to trade calls or puts, you must pull up an option chain to determine which option you will trade. An option chain is essentially a list of all the puts and calls available for the particular stock in which you are interested.

Now, that wasn't so hard to understand, was it? The confusing part comes when you pull up a stock option chain to review.

View By Expiration: <u>Aug 09</u> | <u>Sep 09</u> | **Dec 09** | <u>Jan 10</u> | <u>Mar 10</u> | <u>Jan 11</u>

CALL OPTIONS   Expire at close Fri, Dec 18, 2009

Strike	Symbol	Last	Chg	Bid	Ask	Vol	Open Int
25.00	MVLLE.X	14.00	0.00	14.00	14.20	5	18
30.00	MVLLF.X	9.20	0.00	9.40	9.60	69	165
35.00	MVLLG.X	5.80	0.00	5.40	5.60	12	504
40.00	MVLLH.X	2.25	0.00	2.45	2.55	12	431
45.00	MVLLI.X	0.80	⬆ 0.10	0.80	0.90	55	1,111
50.00	MVLLJ.X	0.20	0.00	0.15	0.25	10	28

PUT OPTIONS   Expire at close Fri, Dec 18, 2009

Strike	Symbol	Last	Chg	Bid	Ask	Vol	Open Int
20.00	MVLXD.X	0.12	0.00	N/A	0.15	6	17
25.00	MVLXE.X	0.32	0.00	0.10	0.25	10	49
30.00	MVLXF.X	0.65	0.00	0.50	0.60	10	166
35.00	MVLXG.X	1.65	0.00	1.45	1.55	7	6,121
40.00	MVLXH.X	3.70	0.00	3.40	3.60	1	115
45.00	MVLXI.X	5.40	0.00	6.80	7.00	20	20
50.00	MVLXJ.X	9.30	0.00	11.10	11.40	20	30

Highlighted options are in-the-money.

Figure 1.1: A Call & Put Option Chain Source: Yahoo Finance

When you pull up an option chain, all that easy-to-understand information suddenly gets lost in translation, and you're left looking at a table full of numbers and symbols that make absolutely no sense.

Part of the confusion is that every option chain looks different. If you go to Yahoo, CBOE, or your brokerage account and pull up an option quote, you will notice that the layout of each of their chains is entirely different. However, all option chain layouts give the same information regardless of how it is displayed.

Let's walk through the snippet of the option chain listed above, which is a stock option chain of the stock symbol MV:

View By Expiration: Aug 09 | Sep 09 | **Dec 09** | Jan 10 | Mar 10 | Jan 11

CALL OPTIONS						Expire at close Fri, Dec 18, 2009	
Strike	Symbol	Last	Chg	Bid	Ask	Vol	Open Int
25.00	MVLLE.X	14.00	0.00	14.00	14.30	5	18
30.00	MVLLF.X	9.20	0.00	9.40	9.60	69	165
35.00	MVLLG.X	5.80	0.00	5.40	5.60	12	504
40.00	MVLLH.X	2.25	0.00	2.45	2.55	12	431
45.00	MVLLI.X	0.80	↑ 0.10	0.80	0.90	55	1,111

Figure 1.2: An Option Chain of MV: Source: Yahoo Finance

Expiration Months

As you can see from the picture, several different expiration months are listed horizontally across the top of the option chain (Aug 09, Sep 09, Dec 09, etc.). The highlight indicates we are looking at all the call and put options that expire the 3rd week of December 2009.

Some traders want to stay in a trade for one week. Some want to wait for two months, so your trading plan will dictate which expiration month you look at.

Call Options and Put Options

Each stock option chain will list all the calls and puts for the particular stock. Depending on which option chain you are looking at, the calls may be displayed above the puts, or sometimes the calls and puts are listed side-by-side.

Strike

The first column lists all of the different strike prices of the stock that you can trade. An option's strike/exercise price is the price at which the stock will be bought or sold when the option is exercised.

Symbol

The second column lists the ticker/trading symbols. MVLLE.X is the ticker symbol for the 09 December 25 call option. The symbol identifies four things: which stock this option belongs to, what the strike price is, what month it expires, and if it is a call or a put option.

Last

The third column lists the last price at which an option was traded (was opened or closed). It's the price at which the transaction took place. Be aware that this transaction could have been minutes, days, or weeks ago and may not reflect the current market price.

Change (Chg)

The fourth column lists the change in the options price. It shows how much the option price has risen or fallen since the previous day's close.

Bid

The bid price is the price a buyer is willing to pay for that particular stock option. It's like buying a home at an auction. You bid (offer) what you are ready to pay for the home.

Ask

The ask price is the price a seller is willing to accept for that particular stock option. (This is the price the seller is asking for.)

BE CAREFUL: one stock option contract represents or controls 100 shares of stock. So, whatever bid/ask price you see must be multiplied by 100. This will be the actual cost of the contract and is what you will pay when you buy the option.

Volume (Vol)

List how many stock option contracts were traded throughout the day.

Open Interest (Open Int)

This column lists the total number of option contracts still outstanding. These are contracts that have not been exercised, closed, or expired. The higher the open interests, the easier it will be to buy or sell the stock option because it means many people are trading it.

I want the open interest to be 100 or higher for most of the options I trade. There are a few exceptions to this rule, but 100 or more is a good rule of thumb to follow.

Before we move on, let's do a quick recap:

- Buying a call option gives you the right to **buy** a stock, and it makes money when the stock's price increases but in a leveraged fashion.
- Buying a put option gives you the right to **sell** a stock and makes money when a stock's price falls but in a leveraged fashion.

Options trading (the buying side) involves buying contracts that you think will increase in value. Once they rise in value, you sell them at a higher price and pocket the difference. You can profit with them in up, down, or sideways markets.

Stock options contracts are often called derivatives because they are derived from stock prices. The options contracts can be broken down into four components:

1. **Underlying Security**: Options are based on an underlying security (stock). That means each listed stock option is linked to a stock, and the option's price will rise and fall with the stock price. **Not all stocks have listed stock options.**

2. **Right, Not Obligation**: Owning an option gives you the right, but not the obligation, to buy or sell the underlying security (the stock).

3. **Specified Price (Strike Price)**: Listed options have been standardized to represent specific stock prices. The strike is the price the owner will buy or sell the stock for.

4. **Time**: Your right to buy or sell the underlying stock expires on a given date. The period the option exists is also known as the option's life. After that date, the option ceases to exist. The stock does not go away, but the option does.

And we will cover this in depth later, but six factors determine the value of stock options. Six variables that determine what something costs! There are so many moving parts. But as you'll see in a moment with Sam's results, it's worth putting in the time to master this skill!

Now, let's wrap up this chapter with a discussion about opening an account with which to trade options.

DO YOU HAVE AN ACCOUNT APPROVED TO TRADE OPTIONS?

Two common questions for new options investors are, "How much do I need to get started, and how do I open an options trading account?"

You'll likely need to deposit at least $2,500 or more to open the account. That's technically enough to start trading options, but I always encourage people to begin with at least $5,000 to $10,000. You WILL make mistakes, so you need enough money to survive the mistakes.

The good news is the strategy I teach in this book does not require you to use real money or have an options account. However, here are a few tips if you aren't already approved to trade options.

If you already have a brokerage account where you invest, you can contact them to see if they allow trading options. If you don't have a brokerage account, you'll want to search online to find the best options brokers.

Several reputable firms exist, and I have five accounts at different brokers. (I like testing new platforms.) I would list them here, but brokerages are constantly changing, and the information may be outdated when you read this.

With advances in technology, opening a brokerage account is a relatively simple process. Nowadays, they have tutorials to walk you through the process, and if you get stuck, you can always call their customer support and have someone walk you through the process.

Your Investment Objectives

They will ask about your investment objectives (income, growth, capital preservation, speculation, etc.). Note: Options usually fall into the speculation category, but I check all four choices if they allow it.

The Options Agreement

To trade options, you must read and agree to the options agreement. They will also ask questions about your net worth, employment, how many trades you place a year, etc. They are trying to determine how much knowledge and experience you have. The answers to these questions are used to approve or deny your application.

Margin or No Margin

I have a margin account, as it is required for the more advanced strategies I trade, but you don't need one to begin. A simple cash account will suffice. You'll also need to tell them what type of options you want to trade. Request that your broker approves you for buying calls & puts. That's all you will need for the strategies taught in this book.

You may even want to apply for the highest trading level. I prefer that method as I'd rather have the highest trading approval and not need it than need it and not have it. You may eventually learn advanced strategies. If so, you'll already have the authorization. If they deny you, no worries; it's not uncommon. Most investors consider options risky, so some of the more prominent brokers want to ensure you have enough experience. If denied or you don't get approved for the level you want, wait three to six months and apply again. While you wait, you can paper or virtual trade.

That brings us to the secret of Sam and Sara's success. They emailed me, and I swooped in and saved the day (smile). No, I'm just kidding. I didn't do a thing; they deserve all the credit. I showed them a few strategies, and they did all the work to make things happen.

One of the things I showed them was how to paper trade to master the technical aspects of options trading. Once you learn the mechanics, you slowly transition to real money, where you discover how to manage the emotional part of trading options. **Overcoming the fear of losing money and the greed for more is not easy at first.** For this reason, it's best to tackle one skill at a time—mechanics first and emotions second. It's a more cautious and deliberate approach, but the students who follow it have a higher success rate than those who don't.

Sam and Sara followed my process. Remember, their goal was to increase their income fast. Options trading appeared to be a better way of accomplishing that than tying their money up in mutual funds and waiting for their worth to increase. They were also sick and tired of being worried about their financial future. They wanted to control their financial destiny by doing the following:

- earning more income
- spending more time with their family
- giving back to society

Their goal was to earn an extra $2,000–$3,000 per month to supplement their current income. That was their goal, their best-case scenario, but ...

They implemented my blueprint, and their results blew all best-case scenarios into tiny pieces. Naturally, I received an email from Sam.

He told me he had made enough money to remodel his bathroom, re-shingle the roof on his home, buy all new windows for the house, buy a new furnace and A/C, build a fence around the house, and still had enough money left over to equal a 100% increase in his account size.

When I interviewed him, he had just returned from taking a cruise. If you've done the math, that's about $47,540 worth of real value added to his life, and that's on the conservative end. I love happy stories like this.

Disclaimer: All stories aren't so glamorous.

Finally, let me share the secret to Sam and Sara's options trading success with you. It's simple …

1. See how other people did it.
2. Try it for yourself.
3. Adjust according to results.
4. Rinse and repeat.

You may not know this yet, but there is no "new" information about investing. Nada. No secrets. No concepts or methodologies that haven't already been discussed a million times over.

However, what is unique is how information is articulated, distilled, and presented. Students tell me I can simplify complicated subjects. That's why Sam and Sara connected with my website. They said it was the only one that explained things, so they "got it."

Tip: The quicker you understand a topic, the faster you can make money with it.

Remember what I said earlier: To survive in the stock market, you've got to have an edge. But how are ordinary people like you and I ever going to make it? What if you don't have time to trial and error your way to success? Luckily, I found the answer.

It's been around for ages; it's called mentorship. I had a mentor (a rich guy) show me how to do it. You will most likely need a mentor also because the reality is that no one succeeds on their own.

Reading about options trading is great and will move you forward educationally, but I didn't succeed with trading until I paid for someone to mentor me. Said another way, even though I have over $3,000 of free training on the web, I still don't believe you should self-educate and try to learn to trade independently.

I've been investing in options since the late 90s, and I've never met a successful trader who learned how to succeed through books alone! I hope that what you discover in this book will compel you to enroll in more advanced training. That's the purpose of all the free training I put out. I want to inspire people to learn more.

It truly breaks my heart to see a person have to keep working instead of choosing to work. I want to help you get to where you can *choose* to work.

But don't worry, I won't be selling you my coaching services or directing you to a website where the "real" secrets are (smile). Honestly, I don't care who you choose as your mentor; I care that you understand this skill! I want you to experience the trifecta of wealth building:

- earning more income
- having more family time
- giving back to society

With that being said, let's move on. It's time to say goodbye to Sam and Sara so we can focus on YOU. It's time for you to learn the strategies they discovered to see if you can achieve the same level of options trading success. See you in the next chapter!

2

HOW TO BUILD WEALTH
QUICKLY WITH CALLS

"Success in a free country is simple. Get a Job, get an education, and learn to save and invest wisely. Anyone can do it. You can do it."

— WILLIAM J' O'NEIL

I n this chapter, you will discover how to use options to build wealth much faster than traditional buy-and-hold techniques. You could invest thousands of dollars buying stock shares, or for a fraction of the cost, you could instead purchase a call option and double or triple your initial investment. You could leverage your money and turn small sums of money into significant returns. But you don't have to take my word for it.

Later in the book, you'll be able to validate those claims with a proof-of-concept exercise.

THE BASICS

Here's a short review of call options before discussing a few basic strategies.

Buying **call** options gives the buyer the right, but not the obligation, to **buy** shares of a stock at a specified price on or before a given date. Thus, call options increase in value when the underlying stock goes up in price and decreases in value when the stock goes down in price.

___

You buy a call option when you think the underlying stock price will increase. If the stock goes up, you earn leveraged or outsized returns compared to simply buying the stock. If the stock falls or doesn't rise in the time frame you need it to, you'll lose money.

___

Now let's cover a quick example. Imagine you thought the stock IBM would rise in price, so you bought a "17 December 95 call option." This option gives you the right to buy IBM stock for $95 on or before December 17. Now, imagine that IBM comes out with a new product, and the stock goes up to $125.

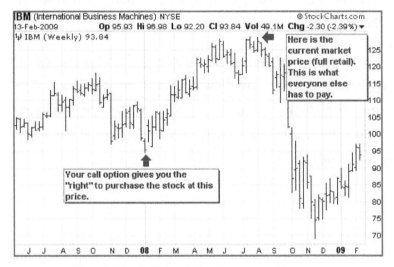

Figure 2.1: Stock Chart of IBM: Source: StockCharts.com

Per the terms of the call option contract, you get to buy the stock for $95. You can purchase the stock at a $30 discount or sales price when everyone else has to pay $125. So as the stock increases in price, the December 95 call option increases in value.

I want you to think back to the real estate example. Remember, we had a contract that gave us the right to buy a home. The home went up in value, so the value of the contract went up as well.

Conversely, call options decrease in value when the stock decreases in price. If IBM falls in price to $75 a share, who wants to purchase a contract that gives them the right to buy IBM at $100 when it's selling for cheaper on the open market?

If you exercised the rights of the contract purchasing the stock at $100, you'd immediately be at a loss of $25 since the stock is trading for $75 on the open market. That's the equivalent of someone trying to sell you a car for $2,000 when the retail value is $1,500.

Risk and Reward

Since there is no limit to how high a stock can rise, the maximum profit you can make with a call option is unlimited. As the stock increases in price, so will the value of your contract.

The max you can lose with a call option is the price you paid for it. If it costs you $500 to buy the call, that's your max loss, which is a lot less money than what you could lose if you bought 100 shares of the stock outright.

Advantages and Disadvantages

+ Advantages

- One call allows you to participate in the upward movement of 100 shares without owning the stock.
- You only have to risk a small sum compared to buying 100 shares.
- The maximum amount you can lose on a trade is the cost of the call.
- You exercise leverage (using a small amount of money to generate outsized returns).
- You will receive higher investment returns if your trade is profitable.

− Disadvantages

- The call option has an expiration date, so you have a limited time to make a profit.
- The stock must move upward for the call to increase in value.
- Options lose a bit of their value each day. Thus, if the stock stays flat or doesn't move, the call option you bought will lose value due to time decay.

HOW STOCK INVESTORS USE CALLS

As a trader of options, you won't concern yourself with exercising the rights of the call contract. You simply want to sell yours for a profit. However, you need to understand how investors use options. This understanding will also help make sense of the technical mumbo jumbo.

Pretend stocks were coming out of a market crash. Everything is cheap and on sale, and you want to buy 100 shares of IBM stock for $95 a share ($9,500). You think the stock has the potential to rise high again, but you are nervous about tying up so much capital because the stock could, theoretically, fall again.

Instead, you buy the "17 December 95 call option" for $5. In reality, it costs $500 as option prices must be multiplied by 100. The $500 is the most you can lose, and it still allows you to lock in that $95 purchase price. In your mind, it's a safer bet than risking the $9,500.

Breakeven Price

Strike Price + Premium Paid = Your Breakeven

In our above example, this equation looks like this:

$95 Strike Price + $5 Premium Paid = $100 (Your Breakeven)

You will recoup your investment paid for the option when the stock reaches $100 a share. Thus, exercising your rights to the call won't make sense unless it's trading for more than $100. However, anything above this price is profit for you.

As stated in our earlier example, the stock shot up in price to $125. Your bet paid off. You were able to test your theory for $500 instead of tying up the entire $9,500. And because you bought a call, you can still purchase the stock at the previous low price of $95.

If you hear someone say that options are risky, I want you to think back to this example. What's riskier? Should you buy $9,500 worth of stock and hope it goes up in price or place a small bet that benefits if the stock goes up but only loses

$500 if it doesn't? In my opinion, options are less risky, but I'm biased. Moving on …

Since the stock went past $100 to $125, you could exercise the "17 December 95 call option" rights and lock in your $20 profit. Let's see if you've been paying attention. What rights do you have as the call owner?

The contract allows you to buy IBM for $95 a share up until December 17th. Since it's an American-style option, you can exercise your rights any time before the option expires.

There are generally two ways options are exercised:

1. You can contact your broker and tell them you want to exercise your option.
2. If the option has value (or it's "in-the-money"), it will be automatically exercised on the expiration day. In our example, it does have value as the stock is higher than the strike of the call.

Since I introduced a new term (in-the-money), let me revisit the six factors that determine the price/cost of an option:

1. the current stock price
2. the strike price of the option
3. the remaining life of the option (time left until expiration)
4. volatility
5. interest rates
6. stock dividends

There are three different terms for describing the strike price of an option as it relates to the stock price.

- Out of the Money: OTM
- At the Money: ATM
- In the Money: ITM

In-the-money options (ITM) have value for the owner of the option. For a call option to be ITM, the stock price has to be <u>above</u> the option's strike price. For a put option to be ITM, the stock price needs to be <u>below</u> the option's strike price.

Here's a picture to help you out:

Option	Strike Price	Stock Price	In, At, or Out of the Money?
Call	45	$40	Out-of-the-money
Call	40	$40	At-the-money
Call	35	$40	In-the-money
Put	80	$100	Out-of-the-money
Put	100	$100	At-the-money
Put	130	$100	In-the-money

Figure 2.2: Out, At, & In the Money Options Examples

Look at the 45 & 40 strike calls. If you exercise those options, would they benefit you? No, you'd be at breakeven with the ATM option and at a loss with the OTM option.

Now, look at the 35 strike call. Do you see how it has $5 of value to the owner since the stock is at $40? So, another way of looking at ITM is in terms of value. If you bought the option and it increased in value (ITM), you could exercise it and make a profit.

ITM options are said to have "intrinsic" or real value. So, the 35 strike call above would have $5 of intrinsic value built into its price (i.e., it would cost more). That's how the strike price affects the options price. The more intrinsic or real value the option has built into it, the more it will cost.

On the other hand, OTM options will be cheaper as they have no real value to someone who owns them and wants to exercise their rights. For example, imagine you owned a $45 strike call, and the stock was trading at $40. If you exercised that call and bought the stock, you'd immediately be at a $5 loss on the stock shares.

Thus, the price you pay for OTM options is comprised of "extrinsic" or time value. Since it has no real value, the market makers put a price on the remaining life of the option, which is what you will pay when you buy it. The time value can also be called a "hope" value. You hope that before the option expires, the stock will move in the direction you need it to move in and build intrinsic value to recoup the cost you paid.

You must understand these concepts, but please remember that most buyers of call options won't exercise their rights because they don't want to buy the stock. They simply want to sell the option contract for a profit if it increases in value. That's what we will be covering in the next section. I'll share the simple 10-minute strategy I taught my wife and young kids.

3

THE BUFFETT CALL OPTION

> ❝ *"The stock market is a device for transferring money from the impatient to the patient."*
>
> — WARREN BUFFETT

Y ou're about to discover the simplest and most profitable trading strategy I've stumbled across. It's a simple trade you place once a year and takes about 10 minutes to set up.

I could reveal it to you here and now, but I've made that mistake before. When I taught the system to members of my coaching program without prepping their minds first, they didn't achieve the same results as me. They kept applying a trader's short-term mindset to a strategy that was designed to be long-term.

That's why the back story is so important. You'll get the intended results when you adopt the same mindset as the person the template is modeled after. Thus, a slight mindset shift needs to happen before you can succeed with this strategy. It's the same mindset shift I had to make before I found success with it.

Here is the shift: **we will trade options like a buy-and-hold investor.** We will use the simple but tedious approach of long-term investors. Maybe like I, you have been told you need special software or technical indicators to succeed as an options trader. After all, you're competing against the best and brightest in the world. You need to know where the market is heading in the short term, right?

Rubbish, I say. I used to think that way because I was brainwashed by successful traders I admired. But one day, I listened to the billionaire investor Ray Dalio speak. He said something that shifted the way I viewed the world.

I can't recall precisely what he said, but the message I walked away with was that I need to learn from successful people with whom I disagree. I needed to study why they believed what they did and then use that to improve my own beliefs.

It was a breakthrough for me. It set me on a journey to learn from investors I had previously dismissed as irrelevant to my trading style—active options trading. In my educational travels, I encountered a relatively unknown fact that would forever change how I traded options.

I've been trading options for over two decades, yet, the easiest and most profitable options strategy I have ever developed didn't come from a trader. And it didn't come from using a bunch of technical indicators and squiggly lines on my stock charts.

No, I modeled it after a billionaire investor who hardly, if ever, uses a computer. By the title of this chapter, I'm sure you can guess who it is. It was Warren Buffett, known as one of the world's wealthiest investors. His company, Berkshire Hathaway, uses options in its overall investment strategy. The public is largely unaware of this because Buffett's options trades are not discussed as much as his opinions on value investing. Yet, Berkshire has made billions from options.

Here is a snippet from the Berkshire Hathaway Inc. 2008 Shareholder Letter:

"Our first contract comes due on September 9, 2019, and our last on January 24, 2028. We have received premiums of $4.9 billion, money we have invested.

We, meanwhile, have paid nothing, since all expiration dates are far in the future."

Trading stock option contracts are often considered risky. Yet, a billionaire investor uses them. So, if it's good enough for him, it's good enough for me.

I affectionally call the above *Buffett's Secret Billion-Dollar Options Trade*, and it's not the only one. There are many others. He uses an options selling strategy beyond this book's scope. Maybe I'll teach that in a book I'm writing about options selling.

However, I want to share a few things I extracted from this trade that helped me with my own buying strategies. I had always been a short-term trader and had never explored any long-term options strategies. Long-term approaches are generally applicable for buy-and-hold investors.

Suppose I'm going to shift to long-term investing. What better person to model than a billionaire investor? That's much superior to learning from a YouTube guru.

Remember what I said about the secret to Sam and Sara's success:

1. See how other people did it. (I discovered how Buffett invested.)

2. Try it for yourself. (I tried the approach myself.)
3. Adjust according to results. (I tweaked and improved the strategy, starting with 1-year options, and eventually moved to 2–3 year options to give myself more time to ride through market corrections.)
4. Repeat.

For nearly 15 years, I had tried the short-term options approach used by many traders, and it worked. But now, it was time for me to try the long-term options approach of a billionaire investor.

With this approach, I buy long-term options and do not care or concern myself with the short-term day-to-day erratic movement of the stock market. I am only concerned about benefitting from the long-term trajectory of American capitalism.

Long-term options are called LEAPS options (Long-term Equity AnticiPation Securities). They enable traders and investors to take advantage of the longer-term trends of the market. Making money with short-term trends is possible but can be tricky as you have to get your timing right. However, profiting from longer-term trends is where the real money is (in my humble opinion).

Before I cover the strategy, let me show you a visual as to why it works so well.

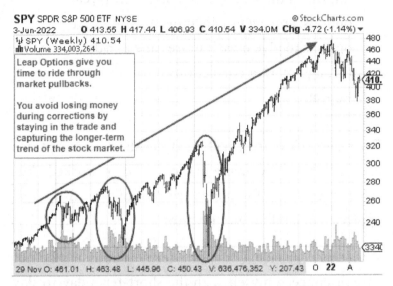

Figure 3.1: A Five-Year Stock Chart of SPY Source: StockCharts.com

Can you imagine waiting five long years to realize the fruits of your labor? Can you see why short-term traders may have a problem with this approach? They get bored and antsy. I often heard this from clients: "Every day, I see the market moving, and I feel like I should be doing something! Am I doing everything right? Is there something else I'm supposed to be doing?"

What was interesting to me as a coach was this. Most people say they want a passive income strategy, but when they get one, it drives them crazy because it's "boring."

If you were programmed with a working-class mentality, passive income could drive you crazy because you have been told that you must work hard for your money. Making easy money feels weird at first! However, you learn to get used to it; over time, it will become hard to return to the old way of doing things.

Enough of my rambles; let's get to the strategy. It's only two simple steps.

THE 10-MINUTE TRADING STRATEGY

You're about to discover how to make money with a strategy that only takes ten minutes of your time. I know how unbelievable that sounds, but it only takes minutes because you're looking at one stock. There is no extensive research involved.

- It only takes ten minutes to place the trade.
- It takes ten minutes to manage the trade.
- And it will take less than ten minutes to close out the trade.

So, when I say it's a ten-minute strategy, I mean it. There's no hype involved.

<u>Before we begin, a quick disclaimer</u>: I am not guaranteeing any income results or saying that success is possible for you. I am merely showing you an example strategy. You are solely responsible for your investment results. Also, when I share my template, I am NOT recommending that you trade the same way I do or use the same stocks I do. I share to demonstrate proof of concept (i.e., this stuff works). If you need advice on what to do with your money, please seek out the services of a registered investment advisor. The information in this book is purely for educational and informational purposes only.

Also, very important: Do not use real money with this strategy initially! The more intelligent approach is to see if you can get a system to work on paper before committing real money. Therefore, I recommend you paper trade this strategy. It's also called virtual trading.

I'll say that in another way, so you know how serious I am about this. You are an absolute idiot if you invest real money before understanding what you're doing.

Abrasive? Offensive? Maybe, but you stop candy-coating the truth when you've seen as many people fail as I have. I won't get into all the reasons why paper trading helps you succeed, but trust my guidance for now. After all, why read a book if you're not going to follow the advice?

That said, I call this strategy the "Buffett Call" because I modeled it after Warren Buffett's long-term options approach. This method can technically be used on any stock, but I prefer using the stock symbols: SPY or SPX. They both track or mimic the S&P 500. The Standard and Poor's 500 (S&P 500) represents 500 leading publicly traded companies in the United States, and it's often used to gauge the overall health or performance of the stock market.

Said more simply, I use SPY (in small accounts) and SPX (in large accounts) because they are more diversified and have less risk and volatility than individual stocks. This stability helps my performance be more consistent and predictable. A stock can drop 20% in one day. It's rare to see the broad-based index (SPX) or the exchange-traded fund (SPY) drop that much in one day; at most, they may drop 5%.

FYI: An exchange-traded fund (ETF) is a marketable security that acts like an index fund but is tradable like a common stock on a stock exchange. So as a trader, if I want to buy and hold shares of the S&P 500, one of the vehicles I can do this through is SPY. Another benefit of SPY that I didn't discover until later in my career is that it can handle "size." Once you start trading with a 6- & 7-figure account, you won't have to adjust your approach. The ETF can manage big money trades. Enough of the intro. Let's move on to the example.

I'll use a hypothetical $50,000 trading account and the historical option prices of SPY on January 4, 2021, and December 31, 2021. I'm not using a template to enter and exit. I'm simply buying a call at the beginning of the trading year, and if it's profitable, I sell it when the year is over. If it's mid-year and I decide to open a new trade, I don't wait; I just enter. Said another way, I do NOT try to time the market.

> **Step 1:** I would invest 20% of my account (10% if I'm being conservative) into the longest-dated December SPY or SPX call option I could buy. It's usually about two to three years out in time. For this example, I will pretend that on January 4, 2021, I purchased two December 2023, 370 call options @ $47.95 per contract. This is called an at-the-money option. It's an option closest to the stock price. Total call Investment: $9,590 (roughly 20% of my account).
> I pick the most extended time frame because it gives me plenty of time to ride through any market corrections that may happen.
> **Step 2:** I leave the rest of my account in cash, uninvested (GASP!)
> "What?! You will leave roughly 80% of your

account in cash? Travis, what's wrong with you? Won't you make more by investing it?"

Yes, young grasshopper, I could make more, but you forget I can also lose more. The #1 rule as an options trader is protecting your capital. Never forget that rule. Jokes aside, there is mental baggage to unpack here, too much, honestly, for the pages of this book. But here is a short mindset lesson.

The people freaking out about keeping so much of my account in cash have not mastered the options game yet. They don't realize that cash is an investment position, and often, it's one of the most profitable positions to be in (think 50% market crash).

People focus so much on how quickly you can make significant gains with options that they forget you can also lose money just as fast. You leave most of your account in cash because you WILL one day lose 100% of your investment in those calls. When that happens, you deploy another 20%.

The biggest secret lies in plain sight: The way to get rich quickly with options is to risk LESS money, not more. You'll understand this point once we review the results of our example trade.

Now, let's fast forward to December 31, 2021. The ETF, SPY, rose 28.8% for the year. That's the buy-and-hold stock return. The SPY call is valued at $126.12 per contract (a 163% increase). Since you bought two contracts, the value of the calls in your account sits at $25,224.

$25,224 - $9,590 (Initial Investment) = Profit of $15,634

We already know the option trade had a 163% increase, which is better than the buy and hold return of 28.8%. However, we didn't invest our entire account, so we need to see how much the overall account grew. We divide the yearly profit or loss by our account value to get this figure. This final number will tell us our percent return on the entire account value.

$15,634 Options Profit / $50,000 Account Value = 31.3% Account Growth

Now let me help you connect the dots here. What you see with this example is the leverage of options. I risked a small amount of money to achieve a much larger profit. In terms of percent return, here is the comparison between the two approaches:

- 28.8% for buy-and-hold, risking <u>100%</u> of your account
- 31.3% for LEAP calls, risking <u>20%</u> of your account

You placed one simple trade and beat the return of buy-and-hold investors while risking less money! Can you understand why someone like me doesn't think options are risky? A few percentage points better may not seem like a big deal, but it adds up over time.

- A sum of $50,000 earning 28.8% a year for ten years, grows into $628,244.
- A sum of $50,000 earning 31.3% a year for ten years, grows into $761,407.

Those few percentage points would add another $133,163 to your account over ten years. Over twenty years, it could add another $3.7 million! Now, do you understand what I meant by the secret to getting rich faster with options is to risk LESS money?

Yes, the high returns are often what initially attract people to trading options, but let me share some wisdom with you. The secret to my success is that I gave up on trying to grow my account quickly. The risk of loss just wasn't worth it. Once I matured and accepted average returns, my accounts started growing much faster, even though a large portion of my money was safely in cash, protected from a market crash.

HYPOTHETICAL BEST-CASE SCENARIO

Since the stock market goes up over the long term, you will most likely win with this approach over time. You may not always have a 163% options return or 31.3% account growth, but if the market does well, you will do well—assuming you stay disciplined and patient (easier said than done).

If you were lucky enough to have a big win like the 2021 example above, you could cash out your profit at the end of the year and repeat.

Another approach I often take is to sell my call once it has reached 100% profit. At this point, you have doubled your money. You WILL be tempted to hold on for even more gains (greed will seduce you). But think about it, you DOUBLED YOUR MONEY!

Do you often get 100% returns in a year with buy-and-hold? Uh, no! So, count your blessings and take your profit off the table. Then, get back in with your profit (smile). See what we did right there?

If you get back in with your profit only, it's still the same dollar amount invested, but it's now money the market gave you. It's not your original investment. If you lose 100% of your money on that trade, did you actually lose money? Some people will say yes, but I think of it as just giving back some of my profit, not losing my original starting amount. That conservative approach has allowed me to survive this options game for over 20 years.

Options aren't risky; people just make risky decisions. Most people are too greedy to manage options correctly. They were created to protect against risk, but people use them to increase their risk (i.e., make more money). It's no different from cars. Cars are not inherently dangerous, but if you drive one like an idiot, then driving is risky.

HYPOTHETICAL WORST-CASE SCENARIO

What if the market crashed like it did in 2007–2009 and took about six years to recover? We usually buy three-year call options, but even those could not survive that crash. You'd lose 100% of the money invested in those calls if that happened. A 100% loss is a reality every options investor needs to be prepared for. You'd also have to remember that losing 20% of your account would be far better than the buy-and-hold investors' 50%–60% loss.

Since you only allocated 20% of your account, you'd have plenty of money to buy another round of calls. Assuming you are not too scared to do so. The next round would likely be profitable, but if not, you'd have to add more money to your account and keep trying until the market recovers. Or you could quit options, put all your money into buy-and-hold, and wait until the account recovers.

As you can see, this is a simple trade you place once a year. It's *Options Trading Made Simple*! However, very few traders will be able to grow their accounts by 31.3% each year because of their greed and impatience. I know because I've coached thousands of investors. They tell me I'm too conservative, and then they put 40–50% of their account in calls so that it grows faster. They forget all about the losing money part.

At this point, I cease coaching them as I refuse to be a witness to the train wreck about to happen. I've seen that movie thousands of times, and it always ends in a disaster. Putting half of your account in call options is dumb, and if someone wants to be that reckless with their money, I want no part of it.

It's so frustrating for me because I tell every single client why I initially failed with options. I risked too much money on my trades and lost everything. Sadly, some people have to learn the hard way (like me).

Yes, there is a way to put all that cash to work and increase returns, but there is a trade-off. You expose yourself to more risk of loss. However, you mitigate this by using buy-and-hold stock shares instead of options. You can wait for a stock to recover if you lose money. You don't have this luxury with options because they have expiration dates.

In a later chapter, you'll discover a smarter way to increase the 31.3% LEAP/cash return without putting yourself in a position to lose half of your account because of trades gone wrong.

FAQS

Q: *I'm broke and don't have $50,000; what should I do?*

It's not a matter of what you should do; it's a matter of what you're willing to do. I sold my car and all the furniture in my house to raise the capital needed to start trading. My friends laughed at me, and my family thought I needed money to support a secret drug habit (facepalm).

Preaching aside, just start where you are and add more money to your account each year. As of this writing, the average LEAP call I buy costs between $2,000–$4,000. There is no wealth without savings, so you can get into the game once you've saved that amount.

Q: *When the market crashes, can you buy LEAP puts?*

Yes, however, I almost always have one in place for my accounts as I use puts for insurance, peace of mind, and to avoid having to time the market.

Q: *What is the best time to buy the Buffett Call?*

I usually buy my calls in December because more LEAP options are added around that time. In my experience, the trade can be implemented at any time and in any market environment. However, **the BEST time to buy these LEAP calls is during market crashes, which is also the best time to buy broad-based index funds like SPY.** Note: It's also the scariest time to buy them. However, if you purchase calls during a market crash, you'll pay a bit more for them because volatility causes option prices to skyrocket.

In my experience, it doesn't matter if you overpay for the calls. I bought calls for my mom's account during the March 2020 crash. People told me not to because they were overpriced. The result? It nearly TRIPLED her investment when the market went back up. Do you think I cared if they were overpriced when I bought them? If I had listened to the naysayers, I wouldn't have tripled her money.

Q: *What if I don't want to be a long-term trader? Is there a shorter-term template I can use?*

Yes, BUT I don't recommend it. I traded short-term market timing templates for the first 15 years of my career. It works, but it's more challenging and more emotionally demanding. I prefer the long-term set it and forget it strategy just covered. Thus, my current suggestion is that people shouldn't use options to speculate (earn money from short-term moves).

There are more successful buy-and-hold investors than option traders, so it's best to use options like a buy-and-hold investor to have the highest chance of success. But don't blindly believe a word I say. Instead, follow the proof of concept exercise later in the book to validate my suggestions, templates, and earnings examples.

If you are dead set on being a short-term trader, you will need a short-term market timing system. This could be software, a technical indicator, or a simple moving average crossover template.

> **Q:** *It can't be that simple. Do I randomly buy a LEAP call? Don't I need software or a technical indicator to know where the market is heading? What if I buy a call, and then the market crashes?*

Sigh. YES, it is that simple. It's the same process I taught my wife and kids. They don't use any indicators; it's a simple random entry template. They get in at any time and manage it by the numbers, meaning what percent of their account they risk and when they will cash out and capture their profit. If it's good enough for the family of a successful investor, it should be good enough for you.

And NO, you don't need to predict where the market is heading. If the market crashes after you buy, you'll lose money. Duh! There is no need to fear losing money because it will eventually happen; we already planned for this in our template. It's why we risk so little money.

Success with this template is not about prediction; it's about capitalizing on the long-term trend of American capitalism. The one thing you can count on with capitalists is that they will always find a way to make more money. They are driven by profit; it's how they keep score in their game. Thus, we use this to our advantage and ride the upward trend of their business endeavors via the SPY LEAP call option!

To sign up for a FREE video demonstration of this approach, just sign up for the book bonuses: https://www.tradertravis.com/bookbonus.html.

4

WHAT'S THE BEST OPTION TO TRADE?

> *"When money realizes that it is in good hands, it wants to stay and multiply in those hands."*
>
> — IDOWU KOYENIKAN

Let's revisit our ITM, ATM, and OTM options before moving on to your proof of concept exercise. One of the more common questions I receive is, "Travis, which option do I buy?"

There are several approaches to take. Some people like cheap OTM options as they can potentially have outrageous returns of 300% or more.

Some investors like choosing ITM options with a high delta. Delta measures how much an options price will change when the stock moves up or down by $1. Because the option has intrinsic value, the options price will move dollar for dollar with the stock price.

For the Buffett call example, we chose neither ITM nor OTM; we instead bought the ATM call option. Said another way, we chose an option with a strike price close to the current stock price on January 4, 2021.

In my experience, choosing the ATM option is best for beginners. Why? Because it's a simple rule to follow. One of the challenges for new traders is something called analysis paralysis.

Pull up an option chain. You will see hundreds of choices. Some are better choices than others. New traders are often scared of picking the wrong option. Thus, selecting the ATM option gives you the best of both worlds: a decent dollar profit and a good percent return on your investment.

Let me use a quick example to illustrate this point. Below would have been our Buffett call results if we had chosen the ITM, ATM, or OTM call option.

Date: 1-04-2021

- ITM: We buy one "December 2023, 295 call option" @ $94.37 per contract.

- ATM: We buy one "December 2023, 370 call option" @ $47.95 per contract.
- OTM: We buy one "December 2023, 440 call option" @ $18.11 per contract.

For your reference, the ITM 295 call is approximately 40% lower than the stock, and the OTM 440 call was roughly 40% higher than the stock. These were chosen to keep the math simple for our example.

Date: 12-31-2021

- ITM: We sell one "December 2023, 295 call option" @ $188.39 per contract (**a $94.02 profit or a 99.6% ROI**).
- ATM: We sell one "December 2023, 370 call option" @ $126.12 per contract (**a $78.17 profit or a 163% ROI**).
- OTM: We sell one "December 2023, 440 call option" @ $75.42 per contract (**a $57.31 profit or a 316.5% ROI**).

Buying the ITM option would have made more money, BUT it also costs more upfront and has the lowest return on our investment.

Buying the OTM option gave us the lowest profit over-all, BUT it also had the most significant return on investment.

And as I stated earlier, the ATM option gives us the sweet spot in the middle, balancing dollar profit and percent return on investment.

Since I mentioned delta earlier, I want to briefly share the other "Greeks" as they are the last pieces of the options value puzzle I'll discuss. Options fanatics will tell you that you MUST have a thorough under-standing of the Greeks if you want to succeed, but there is one problem. My success proved this statement wrong.

You can imagine my confusion when I was told this because 1.) I was already successful and didn't know about the Greeks, and 2.) My millionaire mentor didn't teach me the Greeks. He was a millionaire and didn't think it was vital for me to master them, so I adopted his attitude.

I'm not saying they are unimportant, but I am saying I was able to succeed without learning options Greeks. Regardless, here is a short intro so that you can at least gain a basic understanding. As you become more experienced, you can develop a deeper understanding if you so choose.

Delta, gamma, theta, vega, and rho are the Greeks. They tell you how four factors (change in stock price, interest rate, volatility, and time) will affect the cost of your stock option. They are the five "what if" scenarios.

For example, what if my stock goes up $5 in price? How much will the cost of my options change? **Delta** will tell you that. A delta of 50 means the options price will increase or decrease by $0.50 for every $1.00 change the stock price makes—up or down.

Gamma measures how much the delta will increase or decrease for every dollar the stock moves. For example, assume gamma is 1.5 and delta is 80. If the stock increases in value by $1.00, the delta will increase from 80 to 81.5.

Theta measures the time value decay of an option. A theta of 0.10 means the time value component of the option loses $0.10 every day that passes. This time value decay (how much your option price declines) is very slow when the option has 3-years left until expiration. However, it speeds up as the expiration date gets closer and falls rapidly during the last 30-days of an options life. Thus, we sell our options long before this happens.

Vega tells you how volatility will affect the options price. Stocks with high volatility have wild up and down price swings, and low volatility stocks have slow and steady price movements. The more volatile a stock is, the higher the options premium will be. The difficulty of predicting stock behaviors commands a higher price for the option because of the additional risk/reward it poses. Simply put, options volatility is a measure of risk/uncertainty.

- high volatility: higher option premium
- low volatility: lower option premium

Finally, **rho** tells you how interest rate changes affect the price. Higher interest rates will increase a call's value and hurt a put's value.

I view the Greeks the same way I view a car's engine. Do you need to know precisely how a car's engine works to drive it? No, you get in and go, and that's how I trade. The LEAP call steps I have already provided tell you how to drive the car. The Greeks tell you what's going on under the hood as you drive. If you want to geek out and study under the hood, have at it. As for me and my house, we simply want to reach our destination.

Said another way, I've seen people nerd out on the Greeks yet fail at trading options. It baffles me, but as my mentor said, "Do you want to feel smart, or do you want to make money?" If you want to make money, then the simple templates you will discover in this book will suffice. It's good to have a general understanding of the Greeks, but you don't need to master them to succeed with my strategies. With other short-term active templates, however, the Greeks are more critical.

In summary, stock options are called derivatives because their value is derived from something else—stocks. The options value or price you pay is comprised of either intrinsic value, time value, or both. Six factors will influence the actual value of the option (already covered), and the Greeks tell you how sensitive the options price will be to various scenarios (speed of the stock's movement, volatility of the stock, the passing of time, etc.).

There you have it: options value simplified! Let's move on to validating this book's profit and income claims.

5

HOW TO TELL IF A GURU IS FULL OF CRAP

> *"The most contrarian thing of all is not to oppose the crowd but to think for yourself."*

> — PETER THIEL

Believe it or not, you already know enough to implement the proof of concept exercise I will teach you.

You buy calls when you think stocks will rise. You will earn leveraged or outsized returns compared to simply buying the stock. If the stock doesn't grow within your time frame, you'll lose all your money.

Now, it's time to verify the above statement. I added this section to the book because of the many questions I get like this:

"Trader Travis, are you for real, man? I've dealt with hundreds of 'trading gurus.' All were scam artists! So, what makes you any different from the rest?"

Short Answer: These results in this book are legitimate and can be yours. If you have access to historical stock and option prices, you can verify the legitimacy of the examples.

Of course, things don't always work out as well in real life because you have the human factor to contend with (greed, fear, etc.). However, you can see the potential if you follow a simple set of rules and let the market do what it does best, go up over time. Unfortunately, it doesn't always go up, which is why we covered the worst-case scenario plans.

Longer Answer: Assume everything I say is full of crap until proven otherwise. Don't believe someone just because they show "proof" (like I try to do as much as possible). Don't believe someone just because they show you their lavish lifestyle. You'd be surprised how many people rent private jets for a photo shoot or have a BMW in the driveway but no food in the fridge.

Don't believe someone because they're charismatic (even psychopaths are charming). Don't believe someone just because they have glowing performance testimonials. Testimonials can be faked and exaggerated. Don't believe someone just because they have no bad reviews online.

So, what can you believe?

In my humble opinion, the only thing you can believe is your own REAL-WORLD experience. Do you want to know if I'm "for real" or if I am a scam artist? It's easy to find out.

Take the information I teach and apply it. Did it work? No? Then don't do anything I recommend.

Seriously, save your money and find someone else from which to learn. The fact is, there are some people for whom my strategies do NOT work. That includes people who are:

- too skeptical
- too greedy
- too afraid to take risk
- too egotistical to follow simple instructions
- not willing to learn

- prone to bail when it gets tough
- playing to not lose instead of playing to win

Those folks are better off learning from someone else. They need someone who will tolerate them; I won't. You can apply this process to anyone.

Is there someone you want to learn from but don't know if they're the real deal? Then apply the advice they give away for free (or buy one of their low-cost products) and use it.

Did it work? Good! If not, move on.

Bottom line: Do what the military taught me, "Trust, but verify!" I dare you (smile).

My opinion isn't putting money in your pocket. YOU need to try something and then decide based on YOUR findings. However, I believe strongly in what I teach and know that it works; I want to help you validate the LEAP strategy. I want to give you a simple system that allows you to see the power (or pitfalls) of options trading.

HOW TO TRUST, BUT VERIFY PERFORMANCE CLAIMS

The following steps are not meant to make you an options trader pro; they were created to help you validate the LEAP call strategy. It's a proof-of-concept paper trading exercise.

As stated before, see if you can get a strategy to work on paper before you commit real money. That's how you separate honest gurus from fake ones. With that being said, let's move on.

This book was written for the general public. The instructions I'm about to give are written assuming you don't have a brokerage account and that you've already read the previous chapters. Please re-read the earlier chapters for clarification if something doesn't make sense.

Finally, these steps were written in 2015, so the website below may change over time. However, this can be done on any site that offers stock charts and options chains.

Step 1: Go to http://finance.yahoo.com/.

Step 2: Type SPY into the quote box and hit go (If they change the website, please find an alternative solution).

Figure 5.1: Yahoo Finance Home Page: Source: Yahoo Finance

<u>Step 3</u>: Pull up a one-year chart of the stock symbol: SPY.

SPDR S&P 500 ETF (SPY) - NYSEArca ★ Watchlist   ✦ Add to Portfolio

204.97 ↓1.13(0.55%) Jan 23, 4:00PM EST
After Hours : **204.52** ↓0.45 (0.22%) Jan 23, 7:59PM EST

Prev Close:	206.10	Day's Range:	204.81 - 206.10
Open:	205.79	52wk Range:	173.71 - 212.97
Bid:	204.07 x 300	Volume:	117,516,753
Ask:	204.73 x 100	Avg Vol (3m):	124,571,000
NAV¹:	204.96	P/E (ttm)²:	17
Net Assets²:	215.91B	Yield (ttm)²:	1.87
YTD Return (Mkt)²:	13.46%		
¹As of Jan 23, 2015		²As of Dec 31, 2014	

1d 5d **1m** 3n 6m **1y** 2y 5y max
click here ➜ customize chart

Figure 5.2: Summary Page of the ETF SPY Source: Yahoo Finance

<u>Step 4</u>: Evaluate the chart. If it's gone up all year (and is still going up), you will buy a call option. If not, pull up a five-year chart; if that's up overall, proceed to the next step.

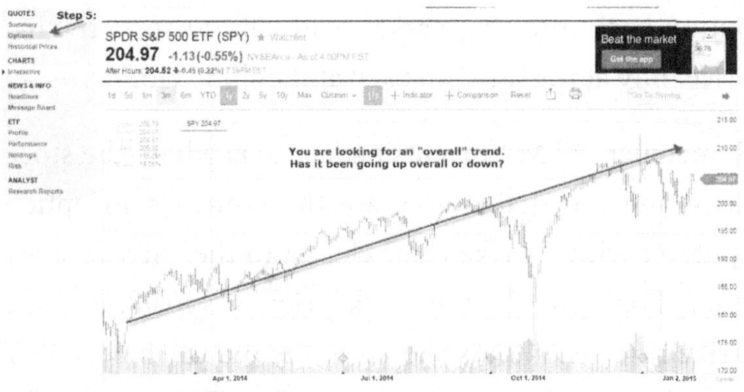

Figure 5.3: One-Year Chart of the ETF SPY Source: Yahoo Finance

<u>Step 5</u>: Look to the top (or top left) and click on the "options" link to go to the option chain.

<u>Step 6</u>: Look for a "date" drop-down menu at the top of the option chain. Choose the farthest dated expiration possible. It's usually 2–3 years out. It doesn't matter when you read this book; just pick the farthest dated expiration available.

<u>Step 7</u>: Refer to step 4. Was the market going up overall? If it was up, then you look at the call options. If not, you still look at the calls and buy one, knowing you may lose money. (This is actually a great lesson to learn on paper.)

<u>Step 8</u>: Find the ATM call option and write down its ask price. You do this because when you're buying an option contract, the ask price is usually what you pay for the stock option. When you are ready to sell that

option back into the market, you will do so at the bid price. Buy at the "ask" and sell at the "bid." Got it?

Remember, ATM (for puts and calls) is where the stock price and the strike price are the same, or an option contract with a strike price closest to the current stock price. For example, the stock price is $40.98, and the strike price is $40. As shown in the picture below, SPY is trading at $204.97, so $205 is the ATM option. The current ask price is $12.09.

Strike	Contract Name	Last	Bid	Ask	Change	%Change	Volume	Open Interest	Implied Volatility
186.00	SPY160115C00186000	21.18	24.68	25.37	0.00	0.00%	2	1587	18.04%
190.00	SPY160115C00190000	22.80	21.68	22.38	0.00	0.00%	70	6426	17.51%
195.00	SPY160115C00195000	18.65	18.27	18.81	0.42	+2.30%	1	8194	16.81%
200.00	SPY160115C00200000	15.10	15.00	15.25	-0.08	-0.51%	1072	23481	15.82%
205.00	SPY160115C00205000	12.05	11.93	12.09	-0.64	-5.04%	1585	15380	15.00%
210.00	SPY160115C00210000	9.30	9.22	9.36	-0.60	-6.06%	833	14352	14.33%
215.00	SPY160115C00215000	7.15	6.79	6.97	-0.02	-0.28%	43	18482	13.65%
220.00	SPY160115C00220000	5.05	4.80	4.97	-0.05	-0.98%	130	6439	13.00%

Figure 5.4: Option Chain of SPY: Source: Yahoo Finance

<u>Step 9</u>: That's it! You just simulated buying a call option.

WHAT TO DO AFTER YOU PLACE YOUR TRADE

So, now what do you do? All you need to do is monitor the trade. Watch it as much or as little as you want and evaluate its progress.

Pay close attention to how much the stock moves percentage-wise versus the option because this shows you the financial leverage we discussed earlier in this book. And remember, you bought at the ask price and will sell at the bid price. The formulas below will help you monitor the trade.

To calculate dollars gained or lost, you'll use the following formula:

(Exit or Bid Price - Entry or Ask Price) * 100 = $ Profit or Loss

Example: $6 - $2 = $4 *100 = $400 Profit

Remember, one option contract controls or represents 100 shares of stock, so the option quote needs to be multiplied by 100 to get the actual cost.

To calculate percentage gains or losses, use the following formula:

(Profit or Loss ÷ Entry Price) *100 = Percent Gain
Example: $400 ÷ $200 = 2 *100 = 200% Return on
Investment (ROI)

———

I know you will be tempted, but there is no daily management or tinkering with the trade! I repeat; leave it alone! You only exit after one of two things happen. You exit any time <u>after</u> your trade hits the 100% gain range or <u>immediately</u> at a 50% loss (give or take).

IMPORTANT: After you exit, rinse and repeat the nine steps. Also, please leave a public review of this book, let me know your thoughts, and share your trading results. Really, leave a review. I get inspired when I see others achieving success with this template.

Sadly, as simple as those nine steps were, this process isn't easy for everyone. It doesn't satisfy any itch to be in the market daily or weekly, and waiting for the exit criteria to be met may bore you to death!

Also, too many people allow their "head trash" to get in the way. **Don't argue with the simplicity of what I**

just showed you. Do it and let the results speak for themselves.

Honestly, you don't have to get rid of any skepticism you may have; only suspend any disbelief temporarily. Let your real-world results speak for themselves.

I wish I could teach only simple strategies, but I've been doing this a long time, and I know newer traders will convince themselves that if they trade more, they will make more. Unfortunately, that is not the truth! Ask any successful trader, and they will tell you.

I teach other strategies to satisfy the needs of those who prefer a more active form of trading. They are more exciting but can be difficult, and you'll encounter more situations where you lose money.

Why? Because the more you enter and exit the market, the more risk you are exposed to. The more straightforward strategies are better for beginners. With my LEAP strategy, you may only place 1–2 trades in a year.

On the other hand, an active strategy of mine once prompted me to place 30–40 trades in one year. I lost money on 17 of them but ended the year up 32%. It was a ton of work. It was like having another job but worth it because I made money.

I don't think many people pursue trading so they can have another demanding job, so consider my suggestion to use passive long-term options strategies. But again, don't believe what I say. Do what the military taught me: trust but verify. Implement the exercise, review your results after 1–2 years, and then decide if this approach is right for you.

Better yet, join me on the beach while our passive trading systems run in the background doing all the hard work. We will be the envy of the 12-monitor trading addicts who can't seem to get away from the market. They promote financial freedom in their sales videos while a gazillion computer monitors sit in the background behind them. How is that freedom? Are you going to take all those monitors to the beach with you? I don't think so.

Compare that to my approach. I don't use several computer monitors. I'm typing this book on the same computer I use to manage a 6-figure portfolio—a $400 laptop I bought from Costco! And when we were driving around the country in our RV or had crappy internet at the RV parks, I switched to trading from my phone.

Enough preaching. I think you get the point. Moving on ...

6

THE SECRET TO BEAR MARKET PROFITS

> *"Rule number one: Never lose money. Rule number two: Never forget rule number one."*
>
> — WARREN BUFFETT

So far, you have seen how buying options can help you build wealth much faster than traditional buy-and-hold methods. But did you know that you can also use option buying to protect your stock market assets from a price decline?

Most investors agonize about how much money they lose when the stock market falls in price. They feel entirely helpless. But did you know there are ways to structure a stock investment so you can't lose money within a specific period?

While some investors feel like victims of market crashes, others are happy and worry-free because they insure their stock portfolios with **put options**. Using this relatively unknown investment tool helps you feel more in control because you can continue making money while stock prices fall.

> Your simple honesty is so REFRESHING...and best of all...it really works! Thanks, Travis. People who want to be successful trading options and don't study your website and join your coaching program simply don't know what they are missing! Here are the first two trades I did using the template ... both winners!
>
> **First Trade (TRLG):** On 8/24, I bought 4 "Oct 20 put options" contracts for $1.85. On 8/30, I sold them for $2.35 (using a trailing stop of $.25 from the mark). My profit was $200; my return on investment was +27% (in only 5 days!!!).
>
> **Second Trade (LULU):** On 8/27, I bought 2 "Dec 36 put options" contracts for $4.90. I sold them for $6.60 (using a trailing stop of $.45 from the mark). My profit was $340; My return on investment was +35% (in only a few days!!!).
>
> -Harry D.

If you recall, I told you that buying put options gives you the right, but not the obligation, to **sell** shares of a stock at a specified price on or before a given date.

A put option will increase in value when the underlying stock declines in price and loses value when the stock rises in price. Slowly read that sentence again. Really, do it.

Most of the people I coach have a hard time wrapping their heads around the concept of making money when stocks fall in price. Don't worry; once I break down how puts work, it is easier to understand the idea.

Remember, put options give you the right to sell stock at a specified price. When you buy put options, you are preparing for, expecting, or wanting the stock price to decline. Imagine hoping for a stock to fall so you can make money. It's so counterintuitive, but that's how these contracts work. Over time you will begin to like bear markets (market crashes) because you make money quickly. Stocks fall more rapidly than they rise.

Now let's go over a few put options examples. If you bought a "May 130, put option" on the stock IBM, the contract gives you the right to sell your IBM shares for $130 on or before the third Friday in May. If your shares' value falls below $130 before then, **you retain**

the right to sell the stock for more than its market value.

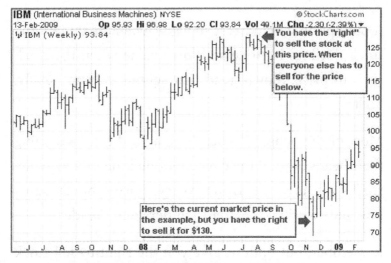

Figure 6.1: Stock Chart of IBM: Source: StockCharts.com

Let's say that IBM falls in price to $75. Everyone else who owns the stock has to sell it for $75, but you own a contract that says you can sell it for $130.

Do you see why put option contracts go up in value as the underlying stock decreases in value? The farther the stock falls below your strike price ($130), the more valuable the option becomes. Essentially, you hold a contract that says you get to sell something for MORE than its market value.

Have you ever been in a losing stock trade and wished you could sell it for more? Or have you ever lost money in an investment and hoped it bounced back in value? If you owned this stock and were facing the pressure of selling it for $75, you would love to have the contractual right to sell it for $130.

But let's say you don't own the stock; you just bought the put option because you thought the stock might fall in price. Do you think that contract has increased in value? Yes, it has, and you can sell it for more than you paid. As I said earlier, a put option will **increase in value** when the underlying stock **declines in price.**

Now let's look at the situation in reverse.

Let's say IBM was trading at $300 a share. Who would want to buy a contract from you that gives them the right to sell the stock for $130 when they could quickly sell it for $300 on the open market? No one. That is why put options decrease in value as the stock increases in price.

Tip: Call options and put options function opposite of each other. So, if you understand how one of them works, it's the exact opposite for the other.

RISK AND REWARD OF BUYING PUT OPTIONS

Put options gain value when stocks fall in price, and there is only so far a stock can sink—the lowest price being $0. A put option's maximum profit is realized when the stock hits this lower threshold.

Put options lose value when stocks rise in price. However, the most you can lose with a put is the price you paid for the contract. If it costs you $500 to buy the put, that's as much as you can lose, which is better than losing thousands of dollars if you purchase the stock and it bottoms out.

Advantages and Disadvantages

+ Advantages

- Puts allow you to profit from the downward movement of the stock without having to own or short the stock.
- You only have to risk a relatively small sum of money to buy a put option, and the maximum amount you can lose on the trade is the cost of the put.
- Puts give you leverage and higher potential investment returns (using a small amount of money to make a large sum).

— Disadvantages

- The put option has an expiration date, so time works against you.
- The stock has to move downward for the put option to increase in value. If the stock stays flat or doesn't move, the put option will lose value due to time decay.

BEAR MARKET TRADE EXAMPLE

<u>Please Note:</u> For this trade and any other example I provide in the book, I will use figures from my broker's historical pricing feature or figures from actual transactions I placed. In a later chapter, you will discover a moving average template that effectively times the market for consistent profits. For now, I want to provide an example of how you could have used the template to buy a put option during the bear market of 2007–2009.

Stock symbol: SPY
On December 20, 2007, you would have received an entry signal to buy a put option. Let's pretend you purchased the "December 2009, 150 put option" for $16.975. Remember, option prices

need to be multiplied by 100 to determine the actual cost, so this would have cost you $1,697.50.

The final exit signal for the trade happened on June 5, 2009 (3 months after the official market bottom). You sold the put at $56.70 for a $3,972.50 gain or a 234% return on your money. As you can see, puts are the secret to bear market profits, and this is one of many examples that demonstrate how market crashes don't have to be bad events. They can instead be opportunities to build wealth.

A non-options trading example of building wealth during a bear market is the 2007–2009 crash; my wife and I increased our 401K contributions to the maximum possible. This caused our accounts to triple once the market recovered. The bear market launched us from financial struggle to financial freedom. That's why it's often been said that more millionaires were created during the Great Depression than at any other time in American history. Most people only hear about the bad stuff that happened during that time; they never hear about all the Great Depression millionaires.

Although it's possible to profit in down markets with puts, I no longer use them this way. Said another way, I rarely trade them to make money anymore. It's honestly too much work as down markets are so volatile. Instead, I use puts for their intended purpose, to act as a hedge or insurance for a stock portfolio. That's what we will cover next!

7

INSURANCE FOR YOUR RETIREMENT ACCOUNTS

> *"Doing the Travis 'Insurance Happy Dance.' We just closed our Insurance PUT for an approximate 113% gain. At work yesterday, some of Annette's co-workers asked her how bad we were getting hurt now that we were doing 'options' in [a falling] market and if she regretted it. She said, 'no, our mentor has taught us how to insure our trades and protect us, and as a matter of fact, we are making money; how are you doing?' Co-worker: Groan and walk off..."*
>
> — BRIAN & ANNETTE

I received the above email during the bear market of 2020. It's a perfect example of the protective power of put options (aka stock market insurance). It's the tool I use to insure all of my investment accounts. It can even be used to insure 401ks, IRAs, etc. I even used puts to protect my mom's TSP government retirement account so that she didn't lose 50% in a market crash.

People buy homes and insure them. People buy cars and insure them. However, after actively investing in the stock market for over 20 years, I am still amazed how many people don't insure one of their most important assets—their stock portfolio! It's unfortunate because stock insurance is cheaper than car insurance.

In my opinion, people don't buy protective puts because of misinformation or, better yet, a lack of information. They simply don't know that it's possible to insure your stock market portfolio. I hope to change that with this chapter. Please spread the word about this fantastic tool, or better yet, fire your money manager if they don't use it!

To be clear, a put is used to profit during bear markets, and a "protective put" is the same tool. The only difference is how you intend to use the contract. Some people buy puts to make money from falling stocks, and others like me use puts for insurance. This practice ensures we won't suffer a crippling account loss during a market crash. Sometimes, we are lucky and make money, but that's never the goal.

SETTING UP THE PROTECTIVE PUT TRADE

To understand this strategy, you must remember that when you own or buy a put option, it gives you the right, but not the obligation, to sell a particular stock at a specified price on or before a specified date.

If you own stocks and buy a put (aka protective put), it acts as an insurance policy. It's no different from the insurance you buy on a house; you protect yourself from an unexpected event. If the house burns down, the insurance company will issue you a check for the home's value. The only money you lost would be the insurance premium you paid. Stock insurance (puts) works the same way.

If you recall, one stock option contract controls or represents 100 shares of the underlying stock. If you owned 100 shares of a particular stock, you'd buy one put to protect those shares. I buy the put with a strike price at or slightly above what I paid for the initial stock. This ensures that if the stock drops in price, I can sell my holdings for precisely what I paid for it or more.

Number of Stock Shares Owned	# of Put Contracts to Buy
100	1
600	6
1600	16
6000	60

Figure 7.1: Protective Put Table: Source: Learn-Stock-Options-Trading.com

Imagine an investor bought 100 shares of XYZ stock @ $90 a share. As protection against a price decline, they also purchase one "XYZ March 90 put" for $2. The stock would have to move up in price beyond $92 for the investor to recoup the cost of the put. That's the tradeoff; the insurance cost eats into your profit. However, speaking from experience, peace of mind is priceless. This is illustrated in the picture below.

Action Taken	Money Out	Money In
An investor buys 100 shares of XYZ stock @ $90	$9,000	
The investor also buys 1 XYZ March 90 Put for $2	$200 ($2 * 100)	
The stock drops to $60/share, the Put is exercised, and the stock is sold for $90 (strike price) **Total Loss = $200**		$9,000 ($90 * 100)

Figure 7.2: Protective Put Trade: Source: Learn-Stock-Options-Trading.com

The purchase of the put guarantees the investor a sales price of $90 for the stock, no matter how far the stock falls in price. The maximum loss is limited to what the investor paid for the put option—$200 ($2 * 100). Without the put, the maximum loss is the entire $9,000! Can you see how puts are an insurance policy to protect your stock from a significant loss?

+ Advantages of Protective Puts

- They allow you to hold on to your stocks and participate in the upside potential while insuring against any losses. You get all the gain of buy-and-hold without the pain of the losses.
- The cost is relatively cheap, considering how much money you are protecting.

— Disadvantages of Protective Puts

- The cost of the put option eats into your profit.
- The put has a limited lifespan (it expires) and must be renewed by purchasing another option.

MANAGING THE PROTECTIVE PUT OPTION

If the stock doesn't drop in value, the put will expire as worthless. If this happens, you can buy another put to continue the protection. When your car insurance policy comes up for renewal, don't you usually renew it? Well, it would be wise to renew your stock insurance as well.

As with any other insurance policy, if you lose money on the put, you should recognize that this is merely the price you pay for protection. If you buy auto insurance and don't have an accident, do you feel cheated, or do you enjoy the peace of mind of full coverage? Living without auto and house insurance is considered unwise, so the same rules should apply to stock investing.

Tip: I never let my puts expire as worthless. I roll them up. As my stocks increase, I sell my old puts (at the lower strike price) and buy new ones at a higher strike (to lock in my gain). Using the example above, if the stock jumped from $90 to $150, I'd sell the $90 strike put and buy a new one at the $150 strike.

At $150, the $90 strike put wouldn't be as helpful. Yes, it would protect your original $9,000 investment, but not your gain. It's like being underinsured. Think houses; when homes go up in value, you should update your coverage or have an inflation rider that does it automatically.

Yes, all this buying and selling of insurance costs money, but I usually obtain my insurance at no cost.

How? I cleverly use call option profits to pay for my puts. You already learned about calls in the previous chapter.

PROTECTIVE PUTS IN THE BEAR MARKET OF 2007–2009

Let me circle back to the bear market put trade I already covered. On December 20, 2007, we bought a "SPY December 2009 150 put option" for $1,697.50. We then sold it on June 5, 2009, for $5,670 (a $3,972.50 gain).

Now, we will add in a stock purchase for the same dates. We bought 100 shares of SPY @ $146.80 a share on December 20, 2007 ($14,680 investment). The bottom fell out of the market, and we sold the stock on June 5, 2009, @ $94.55 a share (a $5,225 loss). As a buy-and-hold investor, you wouldn't sell your stock. I'm just doing it here to compare the stock loss to the option gain.

Our $5,225 loss on the stock and $3,972.50 gain on the put option equals an overall loss of only $1,252.50 or -8.5% of our original $14K stock investment. Without the protective put, we would have lost 35.6% of our $14K investment. I'd take an 8% loss over a 35% loss any day. Selling the put for a profit is the secret back-door method I use to insure traditional retirement accounts like 401ks, IRAs, TSPs, etc. Sadly, most of these accounts don't allow you to trade options.

I have also used this method to insure or protect my mom's TSP retirement account. First, I opened another account. It could be a regular taxable brokerage account or an IRA. I bought enough puts with this second account to insure the stock shares she had in her TSP account. If the market crashed (which it did), I could sell the puts for a profit, which would offset what she lost in her existing retirement account. As you saw in the example above, it's not a perfect solution and doesn't cover 100% of the loss, but it does reduce the loss significantly.

Another option you have instead of using puts, which can be costly, is to use a market timing system where you go to all cash and avoid the market drops. Keep in mind that in a taxable trading account, this will generate significant tax consequences. I prefer to buy my puts at the same time I buy my long-term stock shares. It's easier to keep things in place at all times, and I don't have to stress about making an error with market timing. The downfall is that my puts constantly eat into my profits. This is okay with me as my LEAP calls more than pay for the cost of my protection and even leave some profit left over afterward.

EXERCISING THE PUTS

I'm fortunate because I can trade options in my IRA retirement account. Here is another approach you could take if you owned a protective put in the same account as the shares you are protecting.

Figure 7.2 already showed an example of exercising a put, but let's review it again with this SPY example. I bought the stock @ $146.80 a share and then purchased a "December 2009, 150 strike put" @ $1,697.50. The stock crashed, so I exercised my put.

When you exercise a put, you are exercising the rights of your contract. Said another way, you tell your broker you want to sell your stock at the put's strike price. Exercising a put can be done by calling the broker and informing them of your intentions. Or, in my case, I click the exercise button on my broker platform, and presto, money is put back into my account. I've done it a few times, and the feeling of recouping a loss is priceless. Back to the example:

- You spend $14,680 on the initial stock investment (your account is debited this amount).

- The cost of stock insurance is $1,697.50 (roughly 11% of your total stock investment for two years of peace of mind).
- The stock crashed, so you exercised your put and sold at the put's strike price of $150.
- The broker puts $15,000 back into your account. Your overall loss is only $1,377.50. As you can see, whether you exercise the put or sell your stock for a loss and then sell the put for a profit, the loss is still around the same amount. It's close to what you paid for the put. Again, it's a small price to avoid massive losses during a market crash. And we have already covered a strategy that can potentially pay for the cost of your insurance (the Buffett call).

In my experience, I've never seen an investor concerned about a market crash when put options protect their portfolio. If the stock market falls too low, they either sell their puts for a profit (to offset the loss) or exercise the put and get all their money back.

There is still hope even if you are discovering puts too late and a bear market has already destroyed your account. Like my client Michelle, you can use calls to rebuild your account quickly.

In the financial meltdown of 2008, my accounts were devastated, and I became so exasperated that I called my fund managers. These "professional" investors told me, 'Well, everyone had losses, we all lost money . . . it'll come back.' What really bothered me was the fact that they still charged me tens of thousands of dollars in fees - TO LOSE MY MONEY!

I was extremely frustrated, to say the least, and decided at that moment I had to take control of my money [and learned how to trade options]. I now have the skill to rebuild my retirement account and create a weekly earning FOR LIFE. Needless to say, I have fired all of my "professional funds managers!" In a very short period of time, I have taken what was left of my retirement account and increased it by 163%.

-Michelle F.

If Michelle can do it, you can as well. Her 163% return should make sense if you recall what you learned in the call option chapter. Now, it's time for you to discover precisely how to achieve results like Michelle.

8

INTRO TO THE DMA TEMPLATE

> "*Identical information can lead to opposite conclusions based on relative perceptions of its receivers.*"
>
> — NAVED ABDALI

In an earlier chapter, I tried to convince you that you didn't need special software or technical indicators to succeed with the LEAP call strategy. However, I know there is a segment of traders who are accustomed to using them or who've been programmed to believe you need them.

For those interested, I'd like to share the DMA template. DMA stands for "daily moving average." There are a few versions of the template, but this particular one uses a 200-day simple moving average to signal if it's an excellent time to get into the trade or not. And yes, I'm talking about timing the market.

Market timing is a controversial subject in the investing community. You have one group who says you can't time the market successfully, so you should buy and hold versus getting in and out of the market. The other group swears by market timing and says you make more money timing the market. So, which one is it? Both. You'll find successful investors in both groups, which tells you both methods work.

The approach I explained in my call option chapter was a passive buy-and-hold approach. The benefit of that method is it's simple (i.e., buy a call anytime and risk up to 20% of your account). The downfall of the passive approach is that you will suffer more significant losses when the market declines, which may affect your confidence in the historical fact that the market goes up over the long term. After all, time in the market is more important than timing the market, but despite this fact, people still like to time the market.

So, I'm sharing the DMA template, an active trading approach that uses both calls and puts. With this approach, you'll be better equipped to choose the right time to buy your options. The benefit of the active path is that you avoid losing money in severe market crashes. The negative is that you will have to trade and watch the market more.

Before we get to the ins and outs of the template, let me cover an introductory lesson on stock charts and moving averages for those unfamiliar with them.

HOW TO READ A STOCK CHART

Technical analysis is the formal name for studying or analyzing stock charts. It's used to look at past price behavior and determine where prices are headed in the future.

If you're like my wife, who thinks a stock chart looks like a hospital heart rate monitor, you'll enjoy this lesson. It will help you make sense of all those squiggly lines. Basic charting knowledge combined with other stock indicators can seriously improve your short-term trading skills.

So, what is a stock chart? It's simply a graphical representation of the stock's price over a certain period. When you pull up a chart, there are four primary areas with which to familiarize yourself.

1. Identification Section
2. Time Frame
3. Volume

4. X- and Y- Axis

Let's pull up a chart and go over the key areas. For our example, we will be using Potash Corporation's chart.

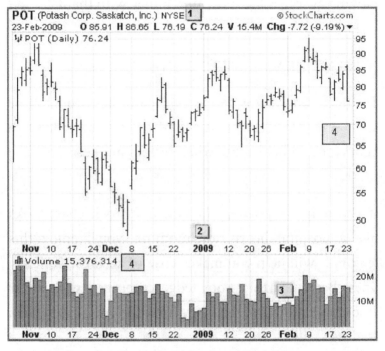

Figure 8.1: Chart of Potash Inc: Source: StockCharts.com

(1) Identification Section

- **Company Name:** Potash Corporation
- **Trading Symbol:** POT
- **Stock Exchange:** New York Stock Exchange "NYSE"

- **Current Date:** 2/23/09
- **Day's Price Change:** opening price is $85.91; day's price high is $86.65; day's price low is $76.19; closing price is $76.24
- **Volume:** On this day, 15.4 million shares of the stock were traded.
- **Change:** This is the day's dollar change compared to yesterday's closing price. So, this stock had a -$7.72 (-9.19%) decline in price from the previous day's closing price.

(2) Time Frame

This chart's time frame is three months. That means it shows us three months' worth of price movement. The time frame can be changed to anything you prefer. For example, with the proof of concept exercise, you looked at a one-year stock chart, but for short-term trades, you may only look at a six-month chart.

(3) Volume

Stock volume measures the number of stock shares that have been exchanged or traded within a specific period. It's how much buying and selling took place during that time. Volume is often called the heart of the stock market because it exposes how much conviction is behind the day's price movement. When you see large spikes in volume, it means many investors were involved in that movement.

(4) X- and Y- Axis

The X-axis runs horizontally across the bottom from left to right. It's the portion of the chart that displays the time frame. The left side is the past, and the right is the present. We use the past as a reference, but we trade from the right side of the chart. We act on what we see now.

The Y axis runs vertically along the right side of the chart. This portion of the graph indicates the price action. For our example, we can see this stock has been in a price range of $50–$95 for the past three months. This is a pretty extensive price range and a highly volatile stock.

Now that you have learned the critical areas of every stock chart, let's go over the three basic types.

- Bar Charts
- Line Charts
- Candlestick Charts

Depending on your trading style, each chart serves its own unique purpose. Bar charts are the most commonly used; Figure 8.1 shows a picture of a bar chart. Line charts aren't used as often, but they are the ones with the squiggly lines I referred to earlier. Candlestick charts are rapidly gaining popularity among traders and have become a favorite of many. I'm a bit old-fashioned; I prefer bar charts.

WHAT ARE MOVING AVERAGES?

A moving average (MA) is a line overlaid on a stock chart that displays the price trend over a certain period. Traders and investors often use them to visualize the market's overall direction. You can also use moving averages as entry and exit signals for your investments, which we will cover in the next section.

You can create a moving average for any time you like (weeks, days, minutes, etc.). Most MAs (like those we will use) are made using the stock's closing price. For example, a 7-day MA is calculated by adding the closing prices for the last seven days and dividing the total by seven.

- $15 + 16 + 17 + 18 + 16 + 18 + 19 = 119$
- $(119 / 7) = 17$

This data point (17) is then plotted on a chart. Tomorrow the same calculation is performed except the oldest day (15) is dropped and a new day (22) is added.

- 16 + 17 +18 +16 + 18 + 19 + 22 = 126
- (126 / 7) = 18

This new point is also plotted on the chart. The latest average price may be slightly different because a new closing price has replaced one of the previous seven closing price points.

As you can see from the example, this stock moves around a bit but trends upward as the average daily price point increases. These calculations are then repeated each day for the selected period.

Again, this is done within any time frame. The weekly MA would use the week's closing price for a particular stock chart. The monthly MA would show you the closing price trends for the month. As the average prices are plotted on the chart, they are connected by a line.

Figure 8.2 shows an example of a 7-day and 30-day MA overlaid on a stock chart.

Figure 8.2: Chart of First Solar Inc: Source: StockCharts.com

The shorter the time, the closer the moving average will mimic price movement. The longer the period, the longer it takes for the average to catch up with the price movement. Hence, all moving averages are called lagging indicators. They lag behind price movement; they always happen after the fact. Notice in the picture how prices are already trending in a specific direction before the 30-day average changes direction.

THREE TYPES OF MOVING AVERAGES

- Simple Moving Average

The simple MA gives equal weight to each price point over the specified period. It's the most widely used moving average and the one I use.

- Exponential Moving Average

The exponential MA assigns more value or weight to recent prices instead of giving equal weight to all. The weighting for each older data point decreases exponentially, giving much more importance to current trends while not discarding older observations entirely.

- Weighted Moving Average

The weighted MA is another moving average emphasizing the latest data, but the calculations are more involved. Weight is assigned to each data point in the average, and each day is multiplied by the assigned weight. The weighted prices are added together and divided by the total number of weights.

In summary, the simple MA is least reactive to price changes, the weighted MA is most reactive to price changes, and the exponential MA is somewhere in the middle. Day traders often use more reactive averages, but since I'm a long-term, passive trader, I will teach you how to use the simple MA to enter and exit your LEAP option trades.

MARKET TIMING WITH THE DMA TEMPLATE

You already learned the mechanics of the LEAP call and put and the risk parameters for options (risking 10%–20% of your total account). Now, you will learn how to time the market with the 200-day simple moving average. We are only using one moving average because it's simple. Focusing on one thing instead of multiple indicators helps avoid analysis paralysis. The 200-day simple MA is best for long-term traders. This way, we avoid buying and selling like short-term traders. Short-term is defined as in and out of trades within weeks.

In my experience, the passive long-term LEAP strategy has the highest success rate. Still, it's also the hardest for newer traders to adapt to as it requires a level of discipline and patience they have yet to develop. But that's also why it works so well; it's fueled by the same habits of the successful buy-and-hold investor the template is modeled after, Warren Buffett.

Let me ask, from whom would you prefer to learn how to trade options? A billionaire investor? Or some guru you found on YouTube? The logical answer is a billionaire, but the reality is that most people learn from free resources online. And what you see online cannot compare to what you can learn from a billionaire. Keep that point in mind if you struggle with the template. Always remember that if you do what rich people do, you are more likely to become rich.

The last point I'd like to make before we get to the entry and exit rules for the template is that this is not what I used to build my wealth, but it is the template I wish I had initially. Short-term options trading was hard, emotionally demanding, and had a considerable time commitment. I knew I couldn't keep that pace up for years. Regardless, I worked hard to build wealth as an active short-term trader, but once I achieved financial freedom, I took my foot off the gas pedal to coast along and enjoy the fruits of my labor. Life is short, so I wanted to enjoy life more. Thus, I searched for a passive way to trade options.

Passive options trading is more manageable, so why take the hard path? Try easy first. Succeed with the DMA template (aka make some money first), and then try to master more complex strategies (short-term trading). Don't you think that's the more intelligent approach? That said, here are the steps to enter and exit trades with the DMA template.

Random Entry Versus Ideal Entry

The following is a random entry template, meaning you can enter a trade at any random time as long as prices are trading above or below the 200-day simple moving average (above for calls and below for puts).

Figure 8.3: DMA Random Entry Example: Source: StockCharts.com

An ideal entry point is five new, obvious price closes above or below the 200-day simple MA. They don't need to be consecutive closes, but they should happen within ten trading sessions (a 2-week time frame). Said another way, if you get five new price closes above the 200-DMA within two weeks, it's a valid signal to buy a LEAP call. It should be a clear price close above the 200-day simple moving average (reverse for puts). If it's a quasi-close above/below that makes you second guess, just wait and evaluate the next day.

We want five new price closes as this signals the stock's long-term trend is potentially changing. Waiting for five means you will avoid most of the fake-out or whipsaw moves, but the tradeoff is that you'll potentially miss some of the profit because you didn't get in on day 1 of the new trend. Again, you'll miss most of the false signals, but as shown in Figure 8.4, you will still experience the occasional back-and-forth signals.

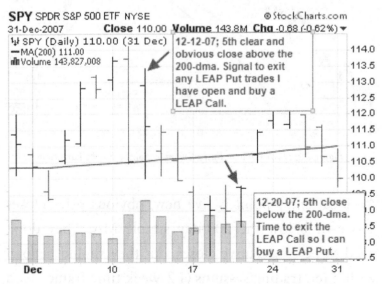

Figure 8.4: DMA Ideal Entry Example: Source: StockCharts.com

As shown in Figure 8.4, the DMA exit signal for the LEAP call option trade is five new, clear price closes BELOW the 200-day simple moving average. And this is when entering a LEAP put option trade is okay. You would exit the put trade once you have five price closes ABOVE the 200-day MA and then buy a LEAP call.

Lastly, I know people will be tempted to wait for an ideal entry, so I have to answer this question. "If you are ready to start a new trade and the ideal entry was a long time ago, do you wait?" **NO!** Don't wait for an ideal entry to enter a new trade! It's a random entry template for a reason; you can safely get into a trade late. If you get in late, you manage the risk of losing money by investing less money than you usually would.

Again, time in the market is more important than timing the market. If you miss a signal or get in late, your risk management and exit signal protect you from losing too much money. Your exit would be a clear and evident price close above/below the 200-day simple moving average.

Once you master your entry and exit, you simply repeat the process of buying calls and puts until you achieve financial freedom! Is it really that simple? Yup! Is it easy? No! Your biggest battle as an investor will be learning how to manage your emotions. Your mental head trash (fear, greed, and doubt) will interfere with the effectiveness of this template. As a coach, I've seen it a million times, but the template works!

PARTING THOUGHTS

Are you getting excited about this LEAP strategy where you place a simple trade roughly once a year? It's a billionaire's approach to trading. OR do you want to be a hyperactive trader chained to the computer screen all day and can't take long vacations because you need to watch your trades? I refer to that as the blue-collar approach to investing, where you feel you need to work hard for your money. Neither approach is good or bad, and everyone has to decide what's right for them.

I started as a blue-collar trader and wouldn't take back the experience or everything I learned. However, now that I'm a husband, dad, and stock market coach, I prefer the passive "set it and forget it" approach to trading options. It allows me to make money but still have a life of freedom.

Now let me show you an example of what life and trading looks like when you use the DMA template.

9

A 15-YEAR DMA CASE STUDY

"Investing should be more like watching paint dry or watching grass grow. If you want excitement, take $800 and go to Las Vegas."

— PAUL SAMUELSON

The following is a long-term case study that includes three significant down periods in the market 2007, 2020, and 2022. I am using the analyze function on the thinkorswim® brokerage platform for the option and stock prices. I'm also using SPY because, in my humble opinion, it's the best stock to trade for most investors. (I already explained why in an earlier chapter.)

I'll start with a fictitious $10,000 account. To keep the math and case study simple, I will simply buy the farthest dated December ATM LEAP call or put option at the time of entry. I will hold it until we get an exit signal (5 price closes above or below the 200-DMA). Since one contract controls 100 shares of stock, I will compare the percentage and dollar return of 100 shares of SPY versus one option contract. I'm only showing the stock loss and gain for comparison reasons. I'm not suggesting you time the market with broad-based ETFs.

The main point of the case study is to show how much money you can make with these LEAP options over time. I'll also provide coaching commentary along the way. It's loosely based on what I've seen while coaching new traders over the last fifteen years. Again, the strategy is simple, but managing your emotions when you experience real-world results is not so easy.

The emotional aspect is precisely why I'm intentionally starting this case study at a nightmarish point. *What if I make a mistake and buy my option right before the market reverses in direction?* It's what everyone fears the most, and it holds them back from implementing. Let's look at what would have happened in 2007 if you had done that.

It's July 2007, the stock market is making new all-time highs, and you feel left out. You have been scared to invest for years because you fear another market crash, like in 2001–2002. To your dismay, the market took off without you, and everyone made money except you. After five years of watching the market go straight up, you can't take it anymore. You decide to get back in. Lucky for you, the market takes a slight dip in August 2007. After some choppy back-and-forth movement, you get a new call option entry point for the DMA template on August 29, 2007.

August 29, 2007: 5th close above the 200-DMA

- SPY closes the day @ $146.54.
- You buy the "December 2009, 150 call option" for $19.60 (roughly 20% of your $10K account value).

You are both excited and nervous. You knew this new adventure wouldn't make you rich overnight, but you secretly hoped it would. You start to imagine what it would feel like to trade full-time. To be free to do what you want, when you want, and with whomever you want.

November 13, 2007: 5th close below the 200-DMA

- The stock sits @ $148.08 ($154 gain).
- You sell the "December 2009, 150 call option" for $20.875 ($127.50 gain).
- You buy the "December 2009, 150 put option" for $17.50.

This reflects only a small gain, but having a win on the first trade was encouraging.

I remember 2007, and you probably wouldn't have trusted the put signal. You might have actually stayed in the call. It depends on how disciplined you were with following templates and how much the news influenced you. The commentary back then was, "Oh, this is just a temporary dip; the market will head back up." They were WRONG.

November 30, 2007: a quasi-close above the 200-DMA that you ignore

December 12, 2007: the 5th close above within the 2-week window

- The stock sits @ $149.37 ($129 gain).
- You sell the "December 2009, 150 put option" for $16.55 ($95 loss).

- You buy the "December 2009, 150 call option" for $20.325.

That trade was a loss, but at least you didn't give back all the profit from your first trade. You remain hopeful. (Remember, puts go up in value when stocks go down in price and decrease in value when stocks go up in price.) Regardless, you aren't too concerned about the loss. You are excited because you think the bull (upward trending) market is resuming.

December 20, 2007: 5th close below the 200-DMA

- The stock sits @ $146.80 ($257 loss).
- You sell the "December 2009, 150 call option" for $17.975 ($235 loss).
- You buy the "December 2009, 150 put option" for $16.975.

You've had to absorb yet another loss. The call and the stock lost money. (Remember, calls go down in value when stocks go down in price and increase in value when stocks go up in price.) At this point, you have been at this for four months, and not only have you given back all your profit, but your account is slightly lower than when you started. Not only are you not rich, but you are losing money! You are annoyed, doubtful, and tempted to look for a new strategy. You feel like something is wrong.

I've seen this story play out a million times as a coach. The disappointment at a loss causes people to abandon the strategy and search for the next bright shiny object or guru promising them easy riches or a guaranteed way to make profits in the market. I know this happens as it happened to me.

If I had stayed committed to my mentor's templates, I would have achieved financial freedom sooner. Instead, it took me over ten years when it should have taken me five, all because I got greedy and distracted. I knew the templates worked because he was a millionaire and used it to make his millions, but knowing and experiencing are two different things. I lacked the faith and commitment needed to succeed. It took me years to develop that. But let's pretend you were committed and faithful and trusted the template.

You decide to follow the template and give it one last try before you abandon it. You choose to trade what you see, not what you think (a big key to success). You reluctantly buy a put, per the template, but secretly hope the put makes up for the loss you just took. The market never recovers and enters into a bear market (a drop of 20% or more that lasted several months).

June 5, 2009: 5th close above the 200-DMA, the end of the bear market

- The stock sits @ $94.55 ($5,225 loss).
- You sell the "December 2009, 150 put option" for $56.70 ($3,972.50 gain).
- You buy the "December 2011, 95 call option" for $15.20.

You stay in this trade for eighteen months and get out roughly three months after the official market bottom. Of course, having the patience to watch your account wiggle around for eighteen months was difficult. And watching some of your profit disappear as the market went up for 3-months was also challenging. However, you followed the template, not your emotions! (Do you see how puts worked in your favor?)

If you didn't experience the bear market of 2007–2009, it wasn't pleasant. I watched both stock and real estate millionaires go bankrupt. Heck, it's when I went bank-rupt from my poor choices in real estate investing. I even heard stories of people committing suicide because they lost so much money. It was an extremely stressful time, and that's putting it mildly. Regardless, it would have been easier for you to suffer through if you had a put in place. The significant profit on the put trade perfectly illustrates this point.

Account value after 2 years: $10,000 + $127.50 - $95 - $235 + $3,972.50 = **$13,770**

After nearly two years of using this LEAP option template, you have made a profit of $3,770, or a 37.7% increase in your account. Simultaneously, the ETF, SPY, has gone down 35.5%. After seeing these results, you are glad you didn't give up after the first few losses. You are also pumped because you can finally see the power of options when you catch a good long-term trend.

A few years later, they have a new December LEAP expiration available. Same rules as before, you buy the farthest dated December expiration. (There is no magic about the December expiration; it's just a simple rule to follow and avoids the analysis paralysis people get caught up in.)

In June 2009, when you enter the call, people are still healing from the bear market pain. Fear and terror are still in the air.

You most likely wouldn't have trusted the signal to buy a call. However, the market doesn't care what we think. It's best to just trade the system and let the results do the talking. Again, trade what you see, not what you think. Moving on...

May 26, 2010: 5th close below the 200-DMA

- The stock sits @ $107.17 ($1,262 gain).
- You sell the "December 2011, 95 call option" for $20.915 ($571.50 gain).
- You buy the "December 2012, 105 put option" for $19.81.

It is a gain, but you aren't happy for some reason. After being in the trade for nearly a year, you have only made $571.50.

This is what I jokingly refer to as a profit snob! Being a profit snob meant you were blinded to the fact that your small gain on this trade was a 37.6% return on your investment in one year. (That's outstanding if you ask me, especially considering that the stock SPY only increased 13.3% in the same period.)

However, the dissatisfaction is normal. Your brain remembered the big win you had after the bear market. The excitement and profit high after a significant gain are like a drug for newer traders. Once you get a taste of the power of options, you can't get enough of it. Your brain seeks the dopamine high again, which is how traders get themselves in trouble. They get bored with small gains and constantly want the big gains. Let me tell you; consistent significant gains are a fairy tale. Learn to be okay with small, consistent profits over time.

June 21, 2010: You ignore the 5th quasi-close above the 200-DMA, waiting for a more decisive close. You never get it within the 2-week window, so you stay in the put trade.

August 6, 2010: 5th close above the 200-DMA

- The stock sits @ $112.392 ($522.20 gain).
- You sell the "December 2012, 105 put option" for $15.465 ($434.50 loss).
- You buy the "December 2012, 110 call option" for $15.885.

August 17, 2010: 5th close below the 200-DMA

- The stock sits @ $109.59 ($280.20 loss).
- You sell the "December 2012, 110 call option" for $15.00 ($88.50 loss).

- You buy the "December 2012, 110 put option" for $19.495.

September 17, 2010: 5th close above the 200-DMA

- The stock sits @ $112.49 ($290 gain).
- You sell the "December 2012, 110 put option" for $17.285 ($221 loss).
- You buy the "December 2012, 110 call option" for $16.155.

What a bummer, three losing trades in a row and a few back-and-forth trades. You are discouraged because your account has dropped a bit lower: $13,770 + $571.50 - $434.50 - $88.50 - $221 = **$13,597.50**. However, it is still higher than the $10K you started with. Thus, you remain hopeful.

August 9, 2011: 5th close below the 200-DMA

- The stock sits @ $117.48 ($499 gain).
- You sell the "December 2012, 110 call option" for $16.45 ($29.50 gain).
- You buy the "December 2013, 120 put option" for $22.015.

January 9, 2012: 5th close above the 200-DMA

- The stock sits @ $128.02 ($1,054 gain).
- You sell the "December 2013, 120 put option" for $15.075 ($694 loss).
- You buy the "December 2014, 130 call option" for $17.195.

Your account is going the wrong way. Two years ago, you were discouraged as your account was getting smaller from its bear market high. As of January 2012, it has shrunk even smaller and you are angry: $13,597.50 + $29.50 - $694 = **$12,933**. The market has been going up for the last three years—up 35.4% since the bear market bottom. When you compare that to your account, doubt starts to creep in, and you wonder if this strategy will work.

You're also having difficulty being patient because it's been almost three years since your last big win. You're annoyed, so you go and complain to a co-worker. This is where you gain some perspective. Your co-worker gets annoyed with you, tells you to stop being a whiny brat, and says he wishes he was in your position. You're confused at first, but then you realize your head trash is blinding you to the facts.

When you started this journey on August 29, 2007, SPY was trading at $146.54. It's now trading at $128.02. It's still down 12.6% from the market high and has not recovered from the 2007–2009 bear market. Said another way, your co-worker's retirement account is still down and showing a loss.

You think about that for a moment. They have watched the market rise for the last three years but haven't made any money yet. Their account is still in recovery mode. Yes, you've given back some of your profit, but at least your account is much higher than where you started. After realizing this, you decide not to quit and press forward with the 130 call option you bought. And good thing you did buy the call because the next trade turned out to be the big winner you've been waiting for.

October 17, 2014: 5th close below the 200-DMA

- The stock sits @ $188.47 ($6,045 gain).
- You sell the "December 2014, 130 call option" for $58.965 ($4,177 gain).
- You buy the "December 2016, 190 put option" for $23.865.

Something shifts for you mentally after this big win. You start to see what your mentor has been saying for years, patience = profits. You notice the pattern; small wins and losses precede the bigger victories. And this small win/loss pattern can continue for years before you achieve significant success. You have been in this trade for nearly three years and are thrilled with your account growth: $12,933 + $4,177 = **$17,110**. This would have been nearly a three-year trade, showing the benefit of the LEAP options. However, the average person would have been unable to sit in that trade for three years and watch that giant gain yo-yo in value. For this reason, I encourage you not to be average; be extraordinary. Decide to develop the patience needed to succeed as a long-term investor.

October 27, 2014: 5th close above the 200-DMA

- The stock sits @ $196.16 ($769 gain).
- You sell the "December 2016, 190 put option" for $20.02 ($384.50 loss).
- You buy the "December 2016, 200 call option" for $15.845.

This was a short-lived put trade. Roughly a week after the last transaction, you got a signal to exit the put and buy another call. And after noticing the small win/loss pattern, you're not even bothered by the loss. You know another significant gain is a few years down the road. However, your patience is about to be severely tested.

August 26, 2015: 5th close below the 200-DMA

- The stock sits @ $194.46 ($170 loss).
- You sell the "December 2016, 200 call option" for $11.56 ($428.50 loss).
- You buy the "December 2017, 195 put option" for $24.54.

October 29, 2015: 5th close above the 200-DMA

- The stock sits @ $208.83 ($1,437 gain).
- You sell the "December 2017, 195 put option" for $18.525 ($601.50 loss).
- You buy the "December 2017, 210 call option" for $18.835.

December 14, 2015: 5th close below the 200-DMA

- The stock sits @ $202.9008 ($592.92 loss).
- You sell the "December 2017, 210 call option" for $15.885 ($295 loss).
- You buy the "December 2017, 200 put option" for $23.28.

March 18, 2016: 5th clear close above the 200-DMA

- The stock sits @ $204.38 ($147.92 gain).
- You sell the "December 2017, 200 put option" for $19.345 ($393.50 loss).
- You buy the "December 2018, 205 call option" for $21.635.

You've had five losing trades in a row, which is hard to deal with from an emotional standpoint. You have been trading from October 27, 2014, to March 18, 2016, with no profits to show for it. Account value: $17,110 - $384.50 - $428.50 - $601.50 - $295.00 - $393.50 = **$15,007**.

Obviously, the template works as your account balance is fifty percent higher than where you started. However, let me ask you a question. After five back-to-back losing trades and nearly two years' worth of trading, would you have the faith to continue using the template?

Wouldn't you start to doubt it? Wouldn't you think it might have stopped working? Then you'd casually research other templates to find something that seems to be working. Can you see that as a normal reaction from someone? I can, and I do see it. But here is the problem.

This situation is EXACTLY why people fail with options! As you can see, the template is simple, and it works. However, the human factor gets in the way. YOU will be your biggest hurdle to success. I know from my own experiences. My template worked, but I got bored and impatient with the slow path to wealth. I then searched for easy riches, and that distraction set me back years. While I was distracted with bright shiny objects (BSOs), my friend Ryan stayed focused on our core template and achieved financial freedom sooner than I did.

I gave up, not knowing what was on the other side of my slow account growth (a big payday). This is also why real-time coaching is so important. A coach can help you through the mental hurdles and compare results with you. If the coach loses money with the same template, you know it's normal. As a coach, I see many people give up when life gets hard. If you want success, you have to push through difficulties. And as you see with the next trade, your patience and faith will pay off.

October 23, 2018: 5th clear close below the 200-DMA

- The stock sits @ $273.61 ($6,923 gain).
- You sell the "December 2018, 205 call option" for $70.165 ($4,853 gain).
- You buy the "December 2020, 275 put option" for $24.415.

Once again, you have another big win followed by several small wins or losses. At this point, you've been trading this template for over a decade. You've traded in up-and-down markets and made money in both. You also see that catching one of these longer-term trades makes slogging through the occasional loss or small gain worthwhile.

However, none of the above applies unless you were one of the few exceptional people who stuck with it this long. If so, your **discipline, patience, and faith** have been rewarded. Having those three qualities is indeed what separates great investors from the mediocre. Moving on…

February 21, 2019: 5th close above the 200-DMA

- The stock sits @ $277.42 ($381 gain).
- You sell the "December 2020, 275 put option" for $21.53 ($288.50 loss)
- You buy the "December 2021, 280 call option" for $31.47.

The market went through a 20% correction between this trade and the last. Then, it rockets higher, which triggers the signal to buy another call option.

March 6, 2020: 5th close below the 200-DMA

- The stock sits @ $297.46 ($2,004.00 gain).
- You sell the "December 2021, 280 call option" for $40.555 ($908.50 gain).
- You buy the "December 2022, 300 put option" for $46.265.

This was the beginning of a short bear market. Do you notice how the cost of the calls and puts increases as the stock increases?

June 2, 2020: 5th close above the 200-DMA (This marks the end of the bear market, roughly three months after the official bottom.)

- The stock sits @ $308.08 ($1,062 gain).
- You sell the "December 2022, 300 put option" for $41.565 ($470 loss).
- You buy the "December 2022, 310 call option" for $35.80.

You bought this call after the market had already experienced a substantial increase. It had already gone up 36% without you! Do you think you could have patiently waited for the signal? Do you see how the human factor or emotions can get in the way?

> All in all, you've been trading this for nearly thirteen years, and managing your emotions is still hard, but it's a little easier now. You now see the rhythm and are okay with it. You wait, wait, and wait to realize a hefty profit. Then, you do it again: wait, wait, wait, and enjoy the profits. After all, the goal is to make money over the long term, and that's what you've been able to do. Account value: $15,007 + $4,853 - $288.50 + $908.50 - $470.00 = **$20,010**.

It took 13 years to double your account (a 100% gain). You averaged 7.7% a year while only investing a small portion of your overall account! That yearly return is close to what buy-and-hold averages each year. Let's see what the stock SPY did in the same period (2007–2020). It started at $146.54 and ended at $308.08. A $161.54 gain or a 110% gain. This could be upsetting until you realize **you risked five times less money than buy-and-hold** and had nearly the same return. Let's cover two more trades before we wrap up this case study.

January 27, 2022: 5th close below the 200-DMA (This is the start of another bear market and within a month of the all-time high.)

- The stock sits @ $431.24 ($12,316 gain).
- You sell the "December 2022, 310 call option" for $129.18 ($9,338 gain).
- You buy the "December 2024, 430 put option" for $60.055.

June 17, 2022: (This is the end of the case study and the lowest market point at the time of this writing.)

- The stock sits @ $365.86 ($6,538 loss).
- Current price of the "December 2024, 430 put option": $77.865 ($1,781 current gain, but the trade would be still open).

Account value: $20,010 + $9,338 + $1,781 = **$31,129**.

You have tripled your account value in 15 years, or a 211% increase (14% a year avg). Buy-and-hold (B&H) had a 149.7% increase (9% a year avg), so now you are beating B&H and still risking less money than required for a B&H approach. With this LEAP option approach, most of your money sat safely in cash, protected from the risk of investing it in the stock market.

Keeping most of your account in cash always drives my clients crazy. They feel that if you invest more, you can make more. It's a normal thought, but most have never been bankrupted like me. Going bankrupt taught me that the downside to risking more money is just not worth it. So, here is my warning: if you get greedy, you will not get rich but will lose all your money. I promise you it will happen eventually.

The way to win with options is to risk LESS money, not more. Options are leveraged and can accelerate your wealth-building efforts (14% a year LEAP options vs. 9% a year B&H). There is ZERO need to be risky. You'll get rich faster if you stay prudent. You don't win by trying to get rich quickly. That's how you lose money. You win by being conservative. The less you invest in options, the more you can make. At least, that's been my experience.

What's also been my experience is that you don't make money in the past. You make money in the present and the future. You can't make money by running a million backtests based on past results. No template is perfect. You eventually have to get out there, make mistakes, tweak, improve, and keep going until you achieve mastery.

BEFORE WE MOVE ON

Over the 15 years this case study took place, was there anything you noticed? What did you learn? Also, does the DMA template allow you to catch the exact tops and bottoms of the stock market? No, nor do you need to. You can make plenty of money catching the middle (the safest) portion of the long-term trend. Did you also notice that you are in call option trades much more than puts? This experience backs up the historical fact that the market goes up more than it goes down.

People stress about down markets, but statistically speaking, they only happen once every so many years. But when they happen, it causes a great deal of emotional pain, and that pain lingers in people's minds for years and makes them scared to invest. However, you no longer need to fear as you know how to trade call and put options successfully.

Whether the market is going up or down, you can prosper. Options, when used correctly, can reduce overall investment risk and even provide a steady stream of retirement income.

To sign up for a FREE video demonstration of the LEAP options approach, just visit: https://www.trader travis.com/bookbonus.html.

10

THE 80/20 WEALTH BUILDING FORMULA

> *"Don't look for the needle in the haystack. Just buy the haystack!"*
>
> — JOHN BOGLE

In this chapter, we will discuss an intelligent way to increase the average 14% a year of LEAP options return without adding more risk by combining traditional buy-and-hold with LEAP options. I initially assumed my mentor would suggest that 100% of my money should be invested in options. Nope! He said that was too risky. He then taught me the 80/20 formula, a more conservative "sleep well at night" approach to building wealth. This strategy ties into my five-year financial freedom plan.

The 80/20 Wealth-Building Formula: Roughly 80% of your money is devoted to long-term buy and hold and 20% to short-term options trading. In a $10K example account, $8K is used to buy shares of the S&P 500, and $2K is used for short-term options trades (buying options & selling options, etc.).

When I first learned this, I thought it was too conservative. I didn't get it. *Why put so little of my money into options? If I commit more of my net worth, won't I get rich faster?*

WELL...after blowing out several accounts over the years, I was like, *Oh, I get it now!* My mentor was right; options are far too volatile. It's best to have a small portion of your net worth devoted to options trading.

That said, here is what the case study results would have been if we combined buy-and-hold plus long-term options trading.

Step 1: First, I'd take roughly 80% of the $10K and invest it all in SPY shares. Using the closing prices of SPY on August 29, 2007, I could have bought 54 shares at the cost of $146.54. That would bring my total investment to $7,913.16. Now that you know about put options and the results of buying puts, there should be no fear of putting your money into buy-and-hold.

Why do we put all of our money into SPY? Because it's simple, and we do not need to diversify because we use options to protect against down markets. Furthermore, according to the SPIVA report (Coleman, 2022), most professional money managers fail to beat the performance of the S&P 500 each year. Thus, in my experience, the best way to beat the pros is to buy the equivalent of the S&P 500.

Step 2: I would invest 20% of my account into the longest-dated December SPY or SPX call option I could buy (the DMA template). As shown in the case study, I purchased one "December 2009, 150 call option" @ $19.60 per contract. This is called an ATM option—an option closest to the stock price. We would pick the most prolonged time frame because it would give us plenty of time to ride through any market corrections that could happen. My total call investment would be $1,960 (roughly 20% of the $10K account value).

The total invested between the two steps would total $9,873.16, with $126.84 left in cash (uninvested). Fast forward to June 17, 2022, and SPY closed @ $365.86. We would have achieved an $11,843.28 profit on our

54 SPY shares and a $21,129 profit on call and put option trades ($32,972.28 in total).

In terms of percentage return, here is the overall account comparison between the two approaches:

- **Pure Buy & Hold:** 149.67% growth, risking 80% of your account (average of 9.97% a year)
- **Buy & Hold With LEAP Calls:** 329.72% growth, using the 80/20 approach (average of 21.98% a year)

Oh my gosh, I'm exhausted now! That was a LOT of math, but here is the simplified summary. With the buy-and-hold plus LEAP option approach, we beat the performance of the S&P 500.

To put this in perspective, let's stretch this out for ten years:

- **Pure Buy & Hold Strategy**: $10,000, which earns 9.97% a year for ten years, will grow into **$25,866.77**
- **Hybrid Strategy:** $10,000, which earns 21.98% a year for ten years, will grow into **$72,926.65**.

Look at the vast difference in those results! Can you now understand why I trade options and will never return to pure buy-and-hold? Are you also excited about the possibilities for your own account now?

Now that you're excited, let's come down from the clouds and talk about reality. Will you most likely earn 21.98% every single year? I have no clue; knowing what types of returns you will make is impossible. I am, however, sharing the blueprint I follow.

The results above are why I tell wannabe options traders not to abandon buy-and-hold. The BEST options traders I have ever seen have the long-term, patient, and prudent mindset of a buy-and-hold investor. It makes sense when you think about it. Look around you. Have you ever seen an options trader on the cover of *Forbes Magazine* as the wealthiest person in the world?

No! You see business owners or long-term buy-and-hold investors. When you first learn options, abandoning buy-and-hold altogether is incredibly tempting. With options, we make better returns while risking less money, but it doesn't come without a price. The price is that options returns tempt you to be greedy. And because they have a limited shelf-life, you can get caught in a trade gone wrong, the options can expire, and you could lose all your money.

So again, don't abandon buy-and-hold. Instead, inte-
grate it with options using the same formula my
mentor shared with me, the 80/20 wealth-building
blueprint. Speaking of blueprints, let's discuss how to
achieve financial freedom in just five short years.

11

HOW TO ACHIEVE FINANCIAL FREEDOM IN ONLY 5 YEARS

> *"I really appreciate all you have done for me! I'm retired now and living debt free. Paid off my home here in Kailua-Kona and a rental triplex home in Honolulu. Now, I'm trading in my IRA account with no stress if a trade is going against me a little...Nice! Mahalo again!"*
>
> — EDWIN O

You've discovered the secret to bear market profits and protecting your traditional retirement accounts against a market crash. You've also been introduced to the DMA template, the billionaire's approach to trading options. Now, we'll take what you have learned thus far and put it into an overall wealth-building blueprint. You'll discover how your newfound knowledge can help you achieve financial freedom in only five years.

For most people, the thought of achieving financial freedom in five years is exciting, but they aren't sure if it's possible. At least, that's how I felt when I was shown this plan. I felt this way until I achieved my goal by following my millionaire mentor's blueprint—the exact blueprint I'm about to share with you in this chapter.

Before I reveal it, let me share my real-world experience so you can see that it's not all rainbows and sunshine on the path to financial independence. Yes, my mentor's blueprint worked, but I failed with it before I succeeded. My failure had more to do with me than the trading templates. I lacked faith in what I was using and didn't stay committed.

I was excited by my initial results but then discouraged by several losses. The disappointment caused me to abandon the strategy. I searched for a guru promising me easy riches or a guaranteed way to make profits in the market. Most veteran traders call this a BSO (bright shiny object). It's something that distracts you from the proven path to wealth creation.

If I had stayed committed to my mentor's templates, I would have achieved financial freedom sooner. Instead, it took me ten years when it should have taken five. All because I got distracted! The sad thing is that I knew the templates worked because he was a millionaire and used them to make millions. But knowing and experiencing it yourself are two different things.

I lacked the faith and commitment needed to succeed; it took me years to develop those traits. Let's assume you are committed and faithful and will trust the blueprint I'm about to share with you. If so, I think you will be thrilled with your results.

THE SIMPLIFIED 5-YEAR BLUEPRINT

You will start with a $10,000 account and grow it by 60% yearly. At the end of 5-years, you will have a six-figure account that should generate enough income for you to live on. Of course, it depends on where you live and how many children you have. The plan also assumes you have no consumer debt like most wealthy people.

Of course, nothing is stopping you from continuing to grow the account. The six figures are just the bare minimum. I'd encourage you to continue growing the account.

If you can continue this 60% growth for ten years, the account will grow into a million dollars, and life becomes more fun when you are trading options with a million dollars.

- Year 01: $10,000 to $16,000
- Year 02: $16,000 to $25,600
- Year 03: $25,600 to $40,960
- Year 04: $40,960 to $65,536
- **Year 05: $65,536 to $104,858**
- Year 06: $104,858 to $167,773
- Year 07: $167,773 to $268,437
- Year 08: $268,437 to $429,499
- Year 09: $429,499 to $687,198
- **Year 10: $687,198 to $1,099,517**

Let me return to the most unbelievable part of the plan —growing your account by 60% a year. Achieving this from trading profits is VERY difficult, so let me show you exactly how my mentor taught me. Spoiler alert: It's not all through investment returns. You can't invest your way to wealth. (I tried but spent it all.) The following is the plan that does work. The first two steps you already know.

Step 1: Allocate roughly 80% of your account to buying and holding SPY shares.
Step 2: Allocate roughly 20% for trading options.
Step 3: Add money to your account on an auto-

mated and scheduled basis. I use the added money to buy more LEAP options, and then if my account strays too far from the 80/20 allocation, I rebalance.

This last step is, in my opinion, the most important and where most people go wrong, including myself. I was taught to be a consumer, so at the beginning of my trading career, I kept spending all my profits, never getting ahead financially. It took me a long time to realize there is no wealth without savings.

I didn't achieve financial freedom until I corrected my consumer behaviors and avoided all consumer debt. In my experience, debt is a big reason people struggle financially. People may not like Dave Ramsey, but his Financial Peace University class changed my life. It took the trading skillsets I already had and enhanced them. That class gave me the missing piece I needed. I needed to truly learn how to live on less than I made and avoid debt which pushed me backward financially. Okay, end of preaching, let's get back to the 5-year retirement plan.

AN EXAMPLE OF WHAT THE JOURNEY LOOKS LIKE

You start with $10,000 and earn the same return as in the case study, 21.98%.

Year 1: Your $10,000 balance earning 21.98% a year in investment returns grows to $12,198 (buy-and-hold plus option profits). If you can save $500 a month, that's another $6,000 you can add to your account. $12,198 + $6,000 = $18,198 (end of first year)

Year 2: Rinse and repeat with the same figures. Your $18,198 grows to $22,197.92. Add in your $6,000 savings, and you will have $28,197.92 at the end of year two.

At the end of year two, you get excited by the results and decide to bump up your monthly savings to $600. You also start adding your $3,200 tax refund into your account each year. For brevity, I'll give you the results for years 3, 4, & 5

Year 3: Your $28,197.92 grows to $44,795.82 (investment returns + personal contributions). By the end of year 3, you've paid off more debt and now bump your savings to $1,000 monthly.

This is in addition to the other factors (tax return + investment returns).

Year 4: Your $44,795.82 grows to $69,841.94 (investment returns + personal contributions).

Year 5: Your $69,841.94 grows to $100,393.20. With an account this size, my wife and I were able to generate between $2,000 to $5,000 a month in income. That was enough for us to live a life of freedom.

Another example. If you initially invest $50,000, making 36% a year, with personal contributions of $500 a month, your account grows to **$293,505** in five years.

Why is the figure significant? After all, it's not the million most people want. Hypothetically speaking, if that $293K account continues to earn 36% yearly, it will produce $105,661 in income. I don't know about you, but that would be enough income for me to quit a job I hated!

Most people think they need a million-dollar account to earn 6-figures a year from the stock market. I just demonstrated how that could be done with a much smaller budget. Selah!

No way it's this simple. It has to be more complicated than this. If you have that thought, it's normal. A little bit of skepticism is healthy.

I, too, was skeptical when I first started. I didn't believe the plan would work, so I quasi-implemented it. After year one, I thought, *CRAP! This does work.* After that, I was all in. My wife and I focused 100% of our efforts on the plan, and after five years of sacrifice, we were able to kiss our corporate careers goodbye, and we haven't been back since.

So yes, it is that simple, but it certainly wasn't easy. There was so much personal baggage and head trash I had to work through in the process (more on this in the next chapter). With that bit of wisdom out of the way, let's talk about best-case and worst-case scenarios.

HYPOTHETICAL BEST-CASE SCENARIO

Since the stock market goes up over the long term, you will most likely win with this approach over time. You may not always earn the 21% to 36% returns shown in the examples, but in my experience, beating the S&P shouldn't be an issue, assuming you stay disciplined and patient (easier said than done).

HYPOTHETICAL WORST-CASE SCENARIO

What if the market crashes like it did in 2007–2009? Well, both your SPY shares and LEAP call would be destroyed. The beauty of stock shares is that they don't expire like options contracts, so you can patiently wait until they recover. But the LEAP call you bought? Yes, they lose money in down markets. That's why you switch to puts to recoup the loss and make money on the way down.

Since the options allocation is only 20% of your account, it won't be financially devasting if you lose on both the call and the put. It will be emotionally devasting for sure but not financially. At this point, you could wait until your buy-and-hold shares recoup the loss or add more money to your account and try again.

This is not the first time I have shared these plans with others. A group of people will always argue with the math or tell you the bazillion reasons why they can't do it. You can argue with the plan, but you can't argue with the results. It simply works!

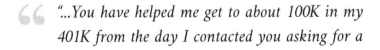 *"...You have helped me get to about 100K in my 401K from the day I contacted you asking for a*

'starting point with options' I will pat you on the back when we meet."

— RASHID K.

This 5-year blueprint worked for the hundreds of traders I have coached and myself. My wife and I didn't have any debt when we hit the six-figure account, which was enough to be financially free.

12

MY RAGS TO RICHES STORY

> *"If I were to say, 'God, why me?' about the bad things that happen to me in life, then I should have also said, 'God, why me?' about all the good things that happened in my life."*

— ARTHUR ASHE- (EMPHASIS ADDED)

I find no joy in talking about myself. I'd rather focus on you and YOUR success journey. However, I'm sharing my story and wisdom in this book for two important reasons.

Reason #1: Options selling gurus inaccurately promote that options buying does not work. Yet, buying options was the key to my success and what I did for the first eight years of my options career. So, my story applies to what's taught in this book.

Reason #2: Transparency is severely lacking in the trading education industry. There are more options trading horror stories than success stories, yet you never hear about them.

Everyone wants to talk about how they turned $2,000 into $100,000 in one year of trading, but hardly anyone talks about how they lost everything. Think about it.

How many gurus (hype merchants) have you seen talk about how much money is lost along the way? Have you ever noticed they have a peculiar habit of only showing you their successful trades? I don't want to do that in this book. I want to show you my wins as well as my embarrassing losses.

You'll be able to see that this journey is not all sunshine and mountains. The valleys of failure are real! But if you don't give up, you may be able to one day achieve financial freedom. That leads us to my story.

The media will focus on the fact that I achieved financial independence and retired from corporate America at 34. Then, roughly ten years later, I won the U.S.

Investing Championship. They highlight my wins but gloss over the fact that 90% of my journey looks like failure.

Yes, life is fun now. I live a life of freedom, and the effort to get here was worth it, but there was nothing sexy about my journey. It was long, challenging, and ugly. The majority of my path to financial freedom sucked!

For context, I'll start at the beginning of my journey so you can see how far I have come and how much options trading has changed my life. It will be the abbreviated version of my story, but it is enough for you to see that, although the strategies taught in this book are simple, it doesn't mean the road to wealth will be easy. Let's begin.

HUMBLE BEGINNINGS (BIRTH TO TEENAGE YEARS)

Being an options trader was not what I wanted to be when I grew up. I didn't even know what an options trader was, much less what the term *investing* meant.

We were poor, and poverty was all I had ever known. I grew up in a small town in Virginia. Initially, we lived in a home with no running water or bathroom. Our household toilet was a five-gallon paint bucket we kept in a spare bedroom.

During the day, we used an outhouse as our outside toilet.

There was also a well outside the kitchen door with a hand pump attached; this was our water source.

We heated bath water on the kitchen stove, and all five family members took a bath in this huge galvanized tin tub.

Because of how long it took to heat the water (1-2 hours), we all took a bath in the same water. It was disgusting, but I didn't know any better. To me, this was normal.

We lived in those conditions until I was 10 years old, and then we moved into a home with more modern amenities. However, we didn't move very far up the economic ladder. It was only four of us at this point. My little brother had died a year earlier; he choked on a sandwich at the babysitter's house.

The same year we moved into the new home, we discovered my dad had a brain tumor. I watched my father wilt away, bit by bit, day by day. He died within a year, and our family essentially fell apart. It's easy to remember the day because he died on Valentine's Day, 1989.

GOING DOWN THE WRONG PATH

I spent the next seven years being mischievous and mad at the world. I was abused by a family member, suffered from depression, and had frequent suicidal thoughts. Once, I even tried but failed. We were too poor to afford college, so I got a job at Taco Bell after graduating high school. I hung around others who had no life goal, purpose, or vision for their life. We were just trying to survive the jungle of the streets.

Eventually, my cousin and I found ourselves in the middle of a shootout. My car was shot up by a guy who owed us money. He did not like the fact that we had come to collect. I can't recall how many shots were fired, but I do remember where two of the bullets lodged themselves. One landed 2-inches from my head-rest and the other in my gas tank. I never knew a bullet hit my gas tank until a mechanic pointed it out months later. I didn't care about any of it. I had honestly stopped caring at that point.

This path of destruction continued until I was arrested and brought before a judge. I didn't have a lawyer, so I was assigned a public defender. He evaluated my court case and advised that I could avoid jail time if I took positive action to show that I was ready to turn my life around. Reluctantly, I joined the military a week later.

TURNING POINT (AGE 19-22)

The public defender's advice proved to be invaluable. Joining the Army saved my life. For the first time since my father's passing, I had structure, discipline, and a standard to follow. I realized I was tired of being tired, and it was time to change.

I started going to church on base, and that's where I met my first millionaire mentor; he was the pastor. He took me under his wing and began to mentor me. Spending time with him and his family changed my character for the better. He was also the first person to ever talk to me about investing. I had never heard the term before, so I had to ask him to explain what investing meant. He taught me a lot, but I was most intrigued by what he said about real estate.

While still in the military, I applied what the pastor taught me and tried to purchase my first rental property. Although fear caused me to back out of that deal, I continued to educate myself on real estate investing.

Once I left the military, the seed that had been planted sparked an interest that could not be quenched fast enough. All I could think about was making money and becoming financially independent. I managed to buy a few properties, and once the cash flow was sufficient, I quit my corporate job and became a full-time real estate investor. I was quickly amassing my empire.

GREED: A POVERTY MINDSET IS INTRODUCED TO MAKING LOTS OF MONEY

> *"Lust for money brings trouble and nothing but trouble..."*
>
> — 1 TIMOTHY 6:10 (CONTEMPORARY VERSION)

Ignorance, greed, pride, and a poverty mindset are not qualities that will enable you to succeed in life financially, yet I had all of them. Without being versed in sound money management skills, I overextended myself on credit and had no backup plan. I remember thinking *I don't need an emergency fund or 401K. I'm going to be rich!* I dreamed of nothing but mountain tops (success). I didn't factor any valleys (problems) into my plan.

I took every bit of savings I had and poured it all into real estate. Things were going great for the first three years until I encountered my first major problem. Then, I realized how flawed my plan was. It started with one issue and slowly escalated into more.

It took me three years to build up my real estate investing business. It took less than six months for everything to fall apart. It's incredible how that happens! With several homes about to be foreclosed on and zero dollars in the bank, I reached out for help.

CROSSROADS: REAL ESTATE INVESTOR VS. OPTIONS TRADER (AGE 23-29)

I had over $400,000 in debt and was desperate to make money fast, so a friend of mine introduced me to a retired doctor—his options trading mentor. He was a multi-millionaire and had been trading stock options for over 20 years. First, he taught me basic budgeting skills so I would not end up in the same financial mess years later.

The budgeting lessons were a surprise, and I can't say they were welcomed. Argh! I wanted him to teach me how to make quick money, and he was starting with budgeting basics. Looking back, it was the best thing he could have ever done because I'm now using those skills to build wealth instead of spending everything I make. He not only showed me how to make money but also how to keep it.

As my lessons progressed, he eventually taught me about stock options and how to trade them successfully. He was the mentor that taught me how to achieve financial freedom in five years. A vital part of this plan was to get rid of all consumer debt. Once debt-free, I would take a $10,000 account and grow it by 60% yearly. I would have $104,857 in my account at the end of five years, which would generate enough income for me to live on.

Before I continue the story, I want to point out something. At this point, I had everything I needed to achieve financial freedom in only five years. I knew exactly what to do. I wrongly assumed head knowledge was enough. It's not! Success with money is 80% mental and 20% head knowledge or how-to. As you'll soon see, I still failed to achieve my goal despite knowing precisely what to do. Okay, back to the story.

Seeing the power of stock options versus real estate, I sold my car, bought an old 1989 Honda Accord, and used the leftover money to trade options. Also, a good friend and the pastor I mentioned from the military lent me money to prolong the foreclosure process.

Within three months of trading options, I had tripled my account size. I made enough money trading stock options to pay everyone back and sell the homes that were in the foreclosure process. When all was said and done, I still had roughly $130,000 of unsecured debt to pay off from my real estate failure. So, I went all in on options trading.

My early success made me think I was a natural-born pro. At the pace I was going, it was only a matter of time before I became a millionaire. At least, that's what I thought.

In my enlightened, egotistical state of mind, I made a mistake that most amateur traders make. I put my entire account on one trade, trying to get rich fast.

The strategy worked for about two years, and then my habits caught up with me. I crashed and burned. I lost all my money. That happens when you don't listen to people who have succeeded before you.

This time was undoubtedly a low point in my life financially. I went to several lawyers and consumer credit counselors who recommended bankruptcy. I couldn't understand why. I felt it was my debt and responsibility, so I should pay it off, not file for bankruptcy.

I often wonder how things would have turned out if I had become an options trader before I became a real estate investor. Because my mindset was the problem, I probably would have had the same issues. I was programmed for failure.

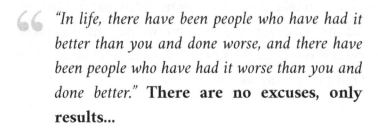

"In life, there have been people who have had it better than you and done worse, and there have been people who have had it worse than you and done better." **There are no excuses, only results...**

— ANTHONY ROBBINS- (EMPHASIS ADDED)

A CHANGE IN DIRECTION

I initially decided against bankruptcy and got a "real" job. I drove a forklift in a Walmart distribution center and made roughly $800 every paycheck. I figured I would be OK with the job and being a part-time options trader. I spent the next four years going through budgeting classes and attending financial seminars. I also read every personal development book I could get my hands on. Tony Robbins, Ken Blanchard, John Maxwell—you name it, I was reading it.

I lived in an empty townhouse, slept in my car when I traveled (I couldn't afford a hotel), and tried to save money any way I could, even if that meant not eating. Things had gone wrong in my life, and at first, I blamed it on my rental units.

However, the more educated I became, and the more books I read, the more I realized that the problem was me. I had to take personal responsibility for my failure. I had no emergency fund, no money management skills, and no idea how to run a business. I was clueless and failing my way to success.

I thought that being an options trader would guarantee me some form of success. After all, I was banking 100%+ winners consistently. I should have made enough money to pay off my debt, but I didn't. My "get rich quick" mindset hindered my success. Once I recognized a pattern, I took some time off from trading.

I hope you didn't miss that point. Being an options trader does me no good if I have the mindset of a poor person or a gambler. I'll just gamble with my money and will ultimately fail. For some, it happens in months, others years. But the road always ends in the same place, failure.

BREAKING POINT

After several years of changing my behavior and mindset and cutting back on my finances as much as possible, I was still over $100,000 in debt. It was so depressing. I wanted some help on my budget and to see if there was anything else I could do. I went back to Consumer Credit Counseling, and after reviewing my budget and debt load, their opinion still had not changed. They recommended filing for bankruptcy.

They finally got it through my thick head that it might take another ten years to pay off my debt, and this was with devoting over half of my paycheck to my creditors.

As a single guy, I was ready for the journey. It took me four long years to take personal responsibility for my situation, and now someone was suggesting I file bankruptcy. I was still hesitant to follow their advice. But things changed.

I met someone that had the potential to be my wife. And once I contemplated getting married, this meant not being able to provide for a family adequately. I couldn't even afford to take my girlfriend out on a date, much less feed any kids we decided to have. There was no way I would make my future wife and family pay for my stupid mistakes.

I reached my breaking point. I struggled with the decision for months, but I finally took the counselor's advice and filed for bankruptcy. Like many, I vowed to pay back the debt eventually. As easy as bankruptcy sounds, I assure you it was not an easy decision. I have to live with that decision for the rest of my life.

THE COURT HEARING

It was hard. I still live with guilt and shame. I've just learned how to manage it better. The whole ordeal was a painful learning experience. I had been someone who never understood bankruptcy or why people filed, yet now I was one of them.

You might envision them skipping away from the courthouse, free from all responsibility. Trust me, no one was skipping away that day! While waiting to be called at the court hearing, I kept my head down so no one could see my tears. In my hand, I held a crumbled piece of paper. On it read the words spoken by Nelson Mandela in one of his speeches, *"The greatest glory in living lies not in never falling, but in rising every time we fall."* Those words comforted me. They helped me get past the humiliation I was feeling.

A NEW BEGINNING (AGE 30 TO 35)

I was pretty numb at this point. I took time to heal and did a great deal of soul searching and asking God for his forgiveness. The pain pushed me in a positive direction. I grew wiser, and eventually, things improved. I found a new job, a new home, and a wife who accepted my past failures. Yes, the same young lady I mentioned above. It was pretty ironic. The new job involved teaching home ownership and financial literacy classes and counseling couples one-on-one.

The clients and all the class participants seem to find the stories about my financial mishaps funny. It certainly wasn't funny at the time. But if I had to go through all of the heartaches to eventually coach people on what not to do, then it was worth it. What's also important to mention is that I barely traded options during this period. The only trades I made were in my mom's account. My options account was emptied as a part of the bankruptcy process.

Furthermore, I inherited nearly $300K of new debt when I married. We were two people who had not mastered the money game. I knew bankruptcy was not the answer, so we took a Financial Peace University class. It changed our life for the better. That class gave me the missing piece I needed. It was the same budgeting skills my millionaire options mentor had given me years earlier. This time, humbled by my failure, I absorbed the lessons taught. Within the next 2–5 years, we paid off all remaining debt, including the mortgage.

We were out of debt and lived in a paid-off 700ft^2 home. We also had no kids at the time. My options mentor had told me to get out of consumer debt, but I didn't listen. That is why I couldn't get ahead financially. I kept spending everything I had made. But once we got out of debt, we used the freed-up cash to build back up my options account. Over the next few years, our net worth exploded.

It's incredible how well you trade when you've been humbled by failure and give up the idea of getting rich quickly. I even joined an options trading group for extra accountability. It felt good sharing my mistakes, especially if it prevented other traders from repeating them.

———

A fundamental fact to mention is that once my wife and I got out of debt, we lived on one person's income and saved/invested the other person's. Ironically, I didn't get wealthy from aggressively trading options like I thought I would. We got rich from having a 60–70% savings rate and conservatively trading options. I know such a high savings rate is unrealistic for most people, so earlier in the book, I provided a plan to follow that still allows you to grow your accounts by 60% each year.

———

After we achieved financial freedom, I kept growing our account and felt confident enough to share my journey with others. That's when I started coaching other traders online. That lasted for about ten years. After helping several other traders achieve financial independence, I decided to retire from active coaching and write books to share my knowledge.

FINAL THOUGHTS

I struggled to write this. The early days of my journey are not parts of my life that I care to relive. But if you're going to learn how to be an options trader from me, I feel it's important to know as much as possible about me—the good, the bad, and the ugly. It's only fair.

It's not easy letting the world see your failures, but there's also a sense of freedom you experience once you stop hiding behind the appearance of perfection. I carry a burden (my failure) that often makes me uncomfortable, but I carry it with dignity!

I'm not perfect, and I've made mistakes. If you're looking for someone who has made all the right decisions, I am not the one. My scars run deep emotionally and financially. Yes, I'm very good at what I do now (being an options trader), but the price I had to pay to get here cost me dearly!

Dreams have a cost. Are you willing to pay that price or not? For some, they succeed, and the price they pay is that they don't have a relationship with their kids. For others, it may be a lifetime of loneliness because they forgot to prioritize dating as they moved up the success ladder. Maybe for some (like me), the only sacrifice is that of time and money. I can't recall who the quote is from, but it went something like this: "Figure out what you want to be in life, pay the price, and then go be it." There will always be a cost to pay!

CONCLUSION

> *"...right now, I know that I have total financial security, and I know that if I lose all my other sources of income, if my husband loses all of his sources of income...I mean, those things are not going to happen...but if they did, I'd be fine. We'd be just fine because I will always make money trading now. I could lose everything else right now, and I'd be just fine. That's a huge peace of mind. That's what everybody wants in life, most people. Everybody wants that, and now I have that, and it wasn't all that hard to get."*

— PATTY

Trading options is simple and highly profitable. You buy a put option when you think stocks will fall in price and a call option when you believe stocks will rise in price. I mean, come on, how hard is that?

It's more complicated than it seems. Primarily, this is due to the human factor of fear and greed. That's why becoming a successful options trader is hard; if it were easy, everyone would be doing it. You have to treat options trading like a business; it takes time, dedication, and much work to build a successful business. That's the truth that hardly anyone wants to tell you!

But if you have the patience to implement what you learn and stick with it until you get your desired results, I think you will find the effort worthwhile. You can be independent of routine and long work commutes and won't have to answer to an incompetent boss. You can live and work anywhere in the world. You can trade from the beach or even a lakeside cabin.

It's a dream lifestyle where you get to make money in up, down, and sideways markets. I've never met any successful trader who regrets how hard it was to make it to the winner's circle. Each week I get emails from people like you sharing how much their life has changed since they learned the concepts taught in this book. Below is a small sample of the notes I receive:

"THANK YOU so much for helping me and teaching these wonderful skills. I have learned so much and applied it to my trading. I have made over $30,000, and I am grateful and blessed that you have shared your teachings with me. Thank you again, and may God continue to Bless you and your family."
-Jody W.

"Over the years, I have never been disappointed by Travis. He has always over delivered on all his promises. I can honestly say he has saved me more money than anyone has in the last 20 years. Notice I said SAVED. 'Risk first, profit second' is his favorite saying, and he taught me to live that way. Making money is a byproduct of that philosophy. My biggest takeaway for me has been mindset. Yes, I have made money and been beating the market consistently. Did I mention he was instrumental in helping me survive the recent crash with flying colors? Travis is the real deal, and I am honored to have him in my life. I look forward to working with him as long as he still wants to teach." -Rashid K.

"So far, I'm up 23% [for the year]...My portfolio average in 3 years is over 70% or so. Only profit... No contributions. This year, I've accomplished more confidence in my trading. Made more monies!! And 2 days ago, I got out of debt entirely. And guess what??

I'm living what you teach!!! Less work (unless you choose), more family time." -Corey C.

Since you've read this far and didn't skip to the back, I believe you also have what it takes to succeed as an options trader. You are now equipped with two proven approaches to trading options—the Buffett call and the DMA template.

Just think, in as little as a few months, you could also be generating these outsized returns compared to simply purchasing shares of stock. However, always keep the risk of loss in the forefront of your mind. If you misuse options, you can lose a great deal of money. Hence, we only allocate 10%–20% of our investment portfolio to stock options.

Even with such a small allocation, the leverage of options can help you achieve financial freedom. Imagine what it would feel like to earn a full-time income from the stock market and live a life free of financial strain. And best of all, you no longer have the dreadful work commute!

- You can work at home in your pajamas (or naked) if you want.
- You can sleep in whenever you want.

- You have enough money to take care of your family.
- You no longer stress about paying bills.
- Your neighbors envy you.

You're set for life financially as you have a skill that allows you to make money regardless of what the stock market does.

You have enough money not only to take care of your loved ones but also enough to give back and tithe to worthy causes. You can help those truly in need. You can do what you want, when you want, and with whomever you want.

That's the life waiting for you once you commit to mastering this skill. Decide today that you will be successful no matter what it takes! Begin your journey toward a wealthy future with options trading. Here's to your success!

A SMALL REQUEST

[+] Don't forget, go to https://www.tradertravis.com/bookbonus.html and get your FREE book bonuses.

[+] If you found value in this book, would you mind taking a minute or two and leaving an honest review on

Amazon. Reviews will help get this book into the hands of people like yourself who want to better their financial future. I also check all my reviews looking for helpful feedback: https://tradertravis.com/otmsreview

REFERENCES

Berkshire Hathaway Inc. (2003). Berkshire Hathaway Inc. https://www.
berkshirehathaway.com/letters/2002pdf.pdf

Berkshire Hathaway Inc. (2009). Berkshire Hathaway Inc. https://berk
shirehathaway.com/letters/2008ltr.pdf

Coleman, M. (2022, March 28). Spiva: 2021 year-end active vs. Passive
scorecard. IFA. https://www.ifa.com/articles/despite_brief_re
prieve_2018_spiva_report_reveals_active_funds_fail_dent_index
ing_lead_-_works/

Dave Ramsey [@DaveRamsey]. (2019, March 7). If you do rich people
stuff, eventually you will be rich. If you do poor people stuff, you will
eventually be poor. [Tweet]. Twitter. https://twitter.com/daveram
sey/status/1103657049689415681

Eagleston, A. (2022, April 8). Options: The scalpel of the financial world.
Forbes. https://www.forbes.com/sites/forbesfinancecouncil/2022/
04/08/options-the-scalpel-of-the-financial-world/

Guziec, P. (2009, April 3). Warren Buffett's comments on option investing.
Morningstar, Inc. https://www.morningstar.com/articles/285699/
warren-buffetts-comments-on-option-investing

Loiacono, S. (2021, January 12). Rules that Warren Buffett lives by.
Investopedia. https://www.investopedia.com/financial-edge/0210/
rules-that-warren-buffett-lives-by.aspx

Rhee, N. (2013, June). The retirement savings crisis: Is it worse than we
think? National Institute on Retirement Security. https://www.nirson
line.org/reports/the-retirement-savings-crisis-is-it-worse-than-
we-think/

The "Win-Win" Strategy Buffett Used To Make $7.5 Million Instantly. (2019,
August 30). Nasdaq. https://www.nasdaq.com/articles/the-win-
win-strategy-buffett-used-to-make-%247.5-million-instantly-
2019-08-30

ABOUT THE AUTHOR

Travis Wilkerson (aka Trader Travis) is the co-founder of the Market- Club Options program and the 2019 United States Investing Champion (Enhanced Growth Division). Travis has mentored thousands of trading students, teaching them the exact strategies he used to reach financial freedom after years of poverty.

You can connect with me on:

https://www.tradertravis.com

twitter.com/tradertravis

Subscribe to my newsletter:

https://www.tradertravis.com/bookbonus.html

Made in the USA
Monee, IL
13 November 2023

46456219R00125